THANKS T°

To Julie Clare & Samuel Becker, for bullying me to start knitting in the first place: none of this would be happening otherwise. It was like an intervention. I didn't know I needed it.

To Will Atkins, for gently telling me when too much is too much. And for the nine-hour Skypes, and for not strangling me.

To Julie Nelson Rhodes, for the design of my brand identity: something so much more than a logo. Such empathy, care, and skill went in, and such elegance, grace, and beauty came out: we knew we needed it on every page.

To Michelle Hazell, who has been with me since the start of my crazy knitting adventure way back when, and whose true friendship I value beyond all measure, calmly giving insights, and sharing her knowledge and expertise, which seemingly know no bounds. I'll keep on being a horror, if you promise to keep on being you.

And most especial thanks to my commissioning editor, Louise McIntyre, who had the vision for this book in the first place, who took a risk on this loose canon, who fought my corner, who talked me down, who dealt with The Tantrum, and who has given me the greatest gift of all: opportunity. I will never be able to fully express the gratitude I feel. I adore you. Thank you.

Nathan Taylor has asserted his right to be identified as the author of this work. All rights reserved. No part of this publication may be reproduced or stored in a retrieval system or transmitted, in any form or by any means, electronic, mechanical, photocopying, recording or otherwise, without prior permission in writing from Haynes Publishing.

First published in October 2018

British Library Cataloguing in Publication Data
A catalogue record for this book is available from the British Library.

ISBN 978 1 78521 199 7

Library of Congress control no. 2018938895

Haynes Publishing,
Sparkford, Yeovil, Somerset BA22 7JJ, UK
Tel: +44 (0)1963 440635
Website: www.haynes.com

Haynes North America Inc.
859 Lawrence Drive, Newbury Park,
California 91320, USA

Printed in Malaysia

While every effort is taken to ensure the accuracy of the information given in this book, no liability can be accepted by the author or publishers for any loss, damage or injury caused by errors in, or omissions from the information given.

Author:	Nathan Taylor [Sockmatician]
Commissioning Editor:	Louise McIntyre
Copy Editor:	Beth Dymond
Technical Editor:	Michelle Hazell
Design:	Will Atkins [WillMakeThings]
Photography:	Will Atkins and Cyrus Mower, Shutterstock
Models:	Jake Watson from Base Models and Sockmatician
Step photos and videos:	Ali Jennings

GUYS KNIT

THE INSTRUCTION MANUAL

FOR THE MAN WITH NOTHING TO PROVE

The Beginner's Guide by
SOCKMATICIAN

CONTENTS

BEFºRE WE BEGIN [CH1]

So what's it all about, this knitting malarkey?

And why should guys be interested in it? The classic 'what's in it for me?' argument.

I'm not sure I can speak for all men. In fact, the only thing I *am* sure of is that I *can't* speak for all men. I can only speak from *this* man's perspective, but I have talked about this very subject with a lot of men over the past few years, and I've been able to draw some conclusions about what appear to be more universal truths.

H°W DID I END UP HERE?

We live in an increasingly digital age. That's a fact that can't be avoided. I know I get twitchy if I can't put my hands on my phone without having to move more than a couple of inches. Conversations don't happen any more without someone reaching for a phone or a tablet to check some sort of fact on Google. Gone are the days where people might—imagine this—actually *discuss* something, rather than simply look it up online and then immediately move on to some other pointless factoid, instantly forgetting the new thing that they have just supposedly 'learnt'. The instant gratification of knowing far exceeds the joy of debate. 'See, I *told* you I was right,' seems to be far more important than engaging in rational argument.

Don't get me wrong: that last paragraph makes me sound like I am some sort of Luddite from the early part of the 20th century, still harping on about the joys of walking ten miles to school in the snow with no shoes on.

Believe me, *nothing* could be further from the truth.

I'm a definite gadget geek. I love technology, and I'm a massive fan of everything that goes with it. (Well, maybe not quite everything—don't write in…) I'd be the last person to say that the digital age we live in is a bad thing.

I used to design websites. (I'm also an actor, and I've appeared in a shedload of musicals in the West End, but that's not relevant to this intro, so park that thought. In fact, forget I ever mentioned it.)

I started looking into web design when the Internet was still a relatively new concept. No one had laptops, and smartphones and tablets didn't exist. HTML was the language of the web, with a bit of JavaScript thrown in. It was laborious and longwinded, and I set about learning it. The coding was clunky, and so pedantic, that even putting the slightest mistake into the programming caused unexpected errors to appear all over your work. You'd then have to spend ages unpicking those errors, and if you couldn't find them, ditching everything and starting all over again.

And I loved it.

I spent untold thousands of hours poring over pages of source code, moving an image on the page to the left by one single pixel, and congratulating myself on how that had utterly transformed the look of the entire website.

But at the end of the day, what did I have to show for my efforts?

A load of ones and zeros, creating pixels of different coloured lights on a screen. Binary code creating… well, nothing.

As soon as the power shuts off, there is… nothing.

I needed something more. I spent all day at my between-acting-jobs day job, staring at a computer screen, and then as soon as I got home, I'd spend all evening staring at a different computer screen, updating my clients' websites. To be frank, I was starting to look a little peaky from not enough exposure to the sun.

I wanted something tangible. Something to reward me for all my hours of hard work–something I could use and keep, long after the power had been switched off.

S°CKMATICIAN

THE SEARCH FºR SºMETHING TANGIBLE

I'm not alone in this. Studies have shown that people all over the developed world are questing for something other than the daily grind of pressing their noses up against their workstation monitors. Hand crafts are seeing something of an explosion, and seemingly long-forgotten, niche techniques are resurfacing like Lazarus, back from the dead. Crafts like furniture making, pottery, and wood whittling are all giving people that sense of practical achievement that has been lacking in their lives for so long. Even, as I recently learnt, an ancient Viking craft of braiding copper wire to make… well… braided copper wire.

So why do we crave this? What is it about making something with our hands that makes us long to bury ourselves elbow deep in a blacksmith's brazier? (That's a metaphor, of course, as actually being elbow deep in *anyone's* brazier is going to hurt like an expletive!)

There are lots of theories. One is that, as a species, we are heading further and further away from the things that link us with the world we live in. On an animal level, we need to reconnect with our environment in a real and fundamental way. One is that it's simply a matter of pride. There is definitely a sense of genuine pride in being able to say—to yourself or to others—look: I made that. I did it all by myself. Then there is the existential argument. We strive to be able to leave a mark, or some sort of dent in the world to show that we were here. We have an urge to leave something behind us that will outlive us, and say to those that follow us:
I achieved something. I mattered. I was here.

I suspect the answer is that they are all true. That there's a little bit of all of them that fuels this need to create.

This is all very well, Nathan, I hear you (rightly) argue, but you still haven't answered the original questions.

Why knitting? Well initially, I answer, 'why not?'

I understand, however, how that might be a little unsatisfactory.

In my case, I had two friends who were very keen knitters, and at about the same time that I was feeling what I now think of as PSDM, or, 'Post-Smartphone Digital Malaise', they had been badgering me to start knitting with them. I asked the exact same question: why? They told me that they thought it would appeal to the way my brain was wired. What utter rubbish, I responded. I have a mathematical, logical brain. The kind of brain that isn't interested in soft furnishings. I like detail, precision, formulas and patterns. Boy-brain attributes.

And there we have it.

Male brain-ness.

Yes, I dropped the gender bomb.

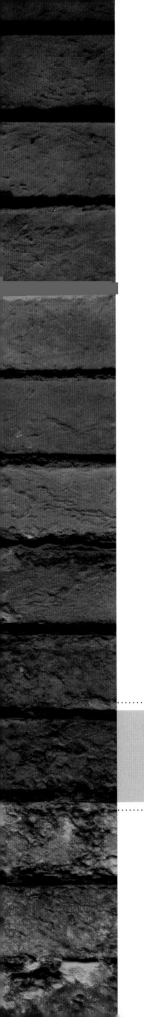

THE GENDER B°MB

It's a difficult subject to bring up, particularly when I work in a predominantly female world. The last thing I want to do is to alienate my female knitting friends and colleagues, many of whom far and away exceed my knowledge and experience in the field.

That said, the fact remains that I *have* noticed differences in the ways that male knitters approach certain aspects of knitting, and I firmly believe that instead of trying to pretend that we are all the same—which we clearly are not—we should embrace the things that make us different, celebrate them, and most importantly, learn from them. *Vive la différence!*

For the rest of this book, then, can it be accepted that when I talk about any perceived differences between men and women, that I in no way suggest that one of these genders is superior to the other? And that obviously, while there are naturally going to be exceptions to every rule, we can't ignore the mathematical phenomenon of the bell curve, whose very form exists to tell us that even though there will always be outliers in any given demographic, the majority of people within it fall in the middle, with a lot of common ground?

Good. That will save me a lot of time trying to craft disclaimers and explanations into anything I might need to say on the matter.

A quick Internet search for 'male brain traits' threw up the following abstract from a research paper by Simon Baron-Cohen from the Autism Research Centre at Cambridge University:

The male brain is a [sic] defined psychometrically as those individuals in whom systemising is significantly better than empathising, and the female brain is defined as the opposite cognitive profile.

Now, before anyone gets on their high horse, this is the first example of what I was just talking about, in terms of bell curves and understanding.

I'm the LAST person to start bandying about gender stereotypes, but there are certain traits that are *traditionally considered* to be male-brain attributes, and some that are *traditionally considered* to be female-brain attributes. (Of course, there will be exceptions to these musings, but that's true of *everything!*)

In simple terms, one could argue that the typical male brain looks for systems in the world around it. It tries to distil the chaos and noise that fills our environments into formulas and patterns that make order and sense of all the hubbub. Men tend to feel secure with logical behaviour, and dare I say it, repeated actions that yield the same results every time. THAT'S a world that makes sense to *this* male-brainer, in any case!

It's a theory that goes a long way to explain why OCD (or CDO, as it should be called, which is alphabetical and therefore MUCH more pleasing...) is so prevalent among men. Or autism, which incidentally, is what the aforementioned research paper is all about—in fact, in the very next sentence, Mr Baron-Cohen goes on to assert that '...autism can be considered as an extreme of the normal male profile'.

But what has any of this got to do with knitting? I'm glad you asked...

WHAT'S IN IT FOR ME?

Knitting is an almost entirely mathematical pursuit. In fact, the Scottish chemist and mathematician, Alexander Crum Brown, used a unique form of three-layer knitting to demonstrate his theories of interlacing and interpenetrating surfaces, and examples of his work can be found in the National Museums Scotland. For the maths geeks among you, he even crocheted a Klein bottle in light blue wool…

Knitting is all about patterns. The very blueprint by which a designer conveys his or her intentions to the knitter is, in fact, even CALLED a pattern! A pattern is a formula, pure and simple. The building blocks of knitting—knit stitches and purl stitches—can be viewed as the ones and zeros of the binary code that creates the end result.

The actions in knitting are small and precise, and repeated with studious and almost obsessive regularity. Attention to detail is key: focus, determination—and sometimes sheer bloody-mindedness—are vital tools for seeing a project through to completion. In fact, James Norbury, British TV knitting expert from the 1950s through to the 70s, even goes as far as to say in the opening paragraphs of his 1968 book, *Knit! With James Norbury*:

> *After forty years' experience of meeting, writing to, and talking to knitters, I have discovered that where many of them fail to give a professional finish to their work, is that they do not pay that meticulous attention to detail that is the essence of good craftsmanship. The fault lies in the fact that learning to knit is so easy and its very ease seems to breed, in the average knitter, a careless attitude that mars the perfection of her finished work.*

Let's allow the fact that he was writing in a book to accompany *BBC Woman's Hour* to have influenced his choice of pronoun at the end. Sanctimonious it may be, but to me, his angle is most definitely that of the quintessential male-brainer. In his day, Norbury was to knitting what Fanny Craddock was to cooking. He even had his own series, *Knit with Norbury*, on the television. He was stern, he was exacting, and he was didactic, but there is no denying he knew his stuff.

And he was a man.

Made from the aforementioned ones and zeros, the knitting-code is long winded and laborious. It is so pedantic that even putting the slightest error into the fabric can cause unexpected mistakes to appear all over your work. You'll spend ages unpicking your mistakes, and if you can't find them you might have to ditch everything and start all over agai—… Hang on a cotton-pickin' minute: isn't all that exactly the same as the stuff I was saying about coding HTML for websites?

Looked at from that angle, knitting consists of all the things that should appeal to your typical male-brainer! Who knew?

It has always astonished me, therefore, that knitting has become very much associated with 'little old grannies' making baby blankets for their grandchildren. I use that term deliberately, even though I find it offensive, because there's definitely a derogatory way in which people view knitting, and by extension, knitters. It is often dismissed as something twee, derisory, and not to be taken seriously.

If you happen to add being a *male* knitter into that mix, well: you are obviously some form of sub-beta-male, soft-handed, nancyish, boy-girl hybrid, better suited to a world of cupcakes, unicorns, and glitter.

Ugh! Stereotypes! (And the people who perpetuate them? *Double* Ugh!!)

One of the main purposes of this book is to challenge and overturn the commonly held perceptions that knitting is only for girls and their grannies.

Yes, it's true that *some* knitters *are* female, and *are* of advanced years, and they *do* enjoy knitting for their descendants. How could that possibly be a bad thing? I celebrate them. They bring with them untold decades of experience and knowledge that you simply can't learn overnight. They 'instinctively' know stuff about the craft (quotes are used because it has taken them a whole lifetime to hone that 'instinct') that I can only hope to know, even if I get to the stage when I've been knitting for as long as they have.

To put this in context, at a class I was teaching in 2017 (on a niche, advanced knitting technique that not everyone knows about), one of my pupils had been knitting for about eighty years. I'm not kidding. She was in her mid-eighties and had been knitting since she was about four or five.

Once she had got her head around the technique that I was teaching, she sped off, way ahead of the rest of the class, with fingers that were working so fast, they looked like they were about to burst into flames. Respect.

At the time of writing, I have been knitting for about seven years. That class was a lesson in humility for me, I can tell you!

But there's so much more to the knitting world than that one single demographic. In my daily life as a knitter, designer and teacher, I come across people from all over the world. Different races, genders, ages. Old and young, male and female, gay and straight, black and white, and every point on the spectra between each of those pairs of adjectives!

You may not know it yet, but the knitting world has evolved. Gone are the days when the only yarn available was pastel-coloured acrylic that squeaked on your needles. Today, the wide variety of bespoke, independent yarn dyers and providers out there allows so much more choice than in days gone by. Knitting is no longer something to be done out of a sense of duty, or under duress, but is instead a high-end, luxury pursuit. This has given rise to the birth of a new breed of knitter, the 'process' knitter, for whom the time spent with needles in hand is as much the end result as the finished object ever could be.

Nowadays, knitting is the domain of the bearded hipster, or the tattooed girl with the facial piercings and the shaved head, just as much as anyone else. Straight men knit for their wives and children. Fathers are teaching their sons how to knit lace shawls for their mothers. I know several men who have knitted socks for their husbands to wear on their wedding day, and girlfriends are encouraging their boyfriends to join them in their favourite pastime.

We knitters often joke that the knitting world is somewhat akin to the wizarding world in the Harry Potter books of J. K. Rowling: we live among you in plain sight, but you have no idea that our world exists, and even if you snatch a glimpse of it, all you will see are processes you cannot comprehend, for you are the uninitiated—the 'muggles', if you will.

And that is what I want this book to go some way towards changing. There is no reason for you to remain the uninitiated. There is no reason for you to think that knitting isn't for you, or that you are the wrong sex to enjoy it.

You are EXACTLY THE RIGHT sex to enjoy knitting, and the structure of your brain would prove that to be true, if you didn't mind me slicing you open to have a closer look!

Knitting, my friend, *is* for you. And when knitting becomes *your* friend, you'll have a friend for life.

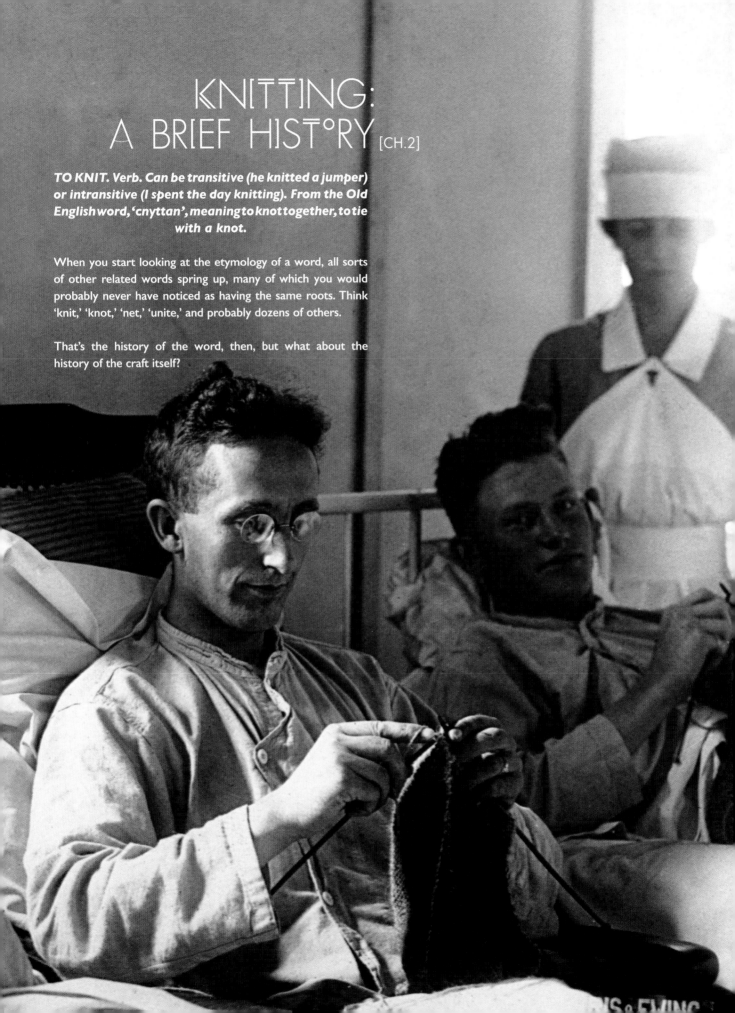

KNITTING:
A BRIEF HISTORY [CH.2]

TO KNIT. Verb. Can be transitive (he knitted a jumper) or intransitive (I spent the day knitting). From the Old English word, 'cnyttan', meaning to knot together, to tie with a knot.

When you start looking at the etymology of a word, all sorts of other related words spring up, many of which you would probably never have noticed as having the same roots. Think 'knit,' 'knot,' 'net,' 'unite,' and probably dozens of others.

That's the history of the word, then, but what about the history of the craft itself?

AN EARLY START

From the research I have been able to do, it seems that there isn't one definitive answer as to when or where knitting was first developed. The very oldest artefacts we have appear to have been made from an earlier technique called nalbinding, or nålebinding. In Danish, it literally means 'needle binding', or 'to bind with a needle'. The process uses a single, flat needle with an eye, rather like a large darning needle, and the maker will create loops of thread in their hands, and will pass the needle through them. There are more similarities with sewing than with the knitting we would recognise today, but it is thought that one may have grown out of the other.

Over the centuries, knitting traditions have sprung up in various places around the world, and it doesn't really seem to be known whether the craft spread out from one single source or developed independently in different places. I would rather suspect it to be the latter, based on the fact that different styles of knitting seem to be more prevalent in certain geographic locations. It is more common, for example, to hold the yarn in the left hand in Scandinavia and other parts of eastern Europe, whereas in the UK, in is much more common to hold the yarn in the right hand. This, of course, could just as easily be the result of different fashions, or different teaching methods, rather than actual discrete discoveries of the technique, but it's certainly food for thought.

20TH-CENTURY KNITTING TRENDS

There was a massive surge in the amount of people knitting during the First World War, as men, women and children on both sides were encouraged to knit hats, socks, jumpers, scarves, and balaclavas for the war effort.

The 1920s saw knitted garments becoming fashionable rather than just utilitarian, with a great taste for jumpers and knitted ties. Whereas knitted jumpers had hitherto largely been made for practical purposes—for fishermen and the like—knitwear was now becoming associated with various sports such as cricket and golf. Prominent figures from the world of high fashion, like the luminaries behind *Vogue* magazine and Coco Chanel also embraced knitwear, bringing it to a whole new audience.

Fashions come and go, but hand-knitted knitwear stayed popular until around the 1980s, when the rise of machine knits and the availability of cheap, synthetic fibres meant that people were less likely to spend their time and money knitting something by hand, when much more cost-effective and easier options were available.

It seemed like the world of the handknit had come to an end.

KNITTING TODAY

But now let's cut to the turn of the 21st century, and the onset of PSDM that I was talking about in the last chapter. (That's Post-Smartphone Digital Malaise, in case you have forgotten.)

The rise of the Internet, and the emergence of online communities that came with it, has meant that people have been able to share and pick up new skills better than ever before. In the past, most people would have learnt how to knit from a parent or grandparent, and their skills would have been limited to what could be passed on from just that one source. Now, we have access to a whole world of knowledge and experience, right at our fingertips, and that explosion of information seems to have fuelled an insatiable thirst for learning that has catapulted this most traditional of crafts right to the forefront of the attention of millions of people around the globe.

It's ironic in a way, that it has largely been the rise of the digital world that has been the catalyst for the rise of interest in knitting, when so many people are returning to knitting precisely to escape the increased digitisation of their world. I couldn't be more grateful for that, though, as I know I wouldn't be sitting here today, typing away on my MacBook Pro, back in the world of ones and zeros, in order to give you the chance to get away from the ones and zeros in your own life, if it hadn't been for the ones and zeros of the online world giving me the opportunity to learn this most time-honoured, historic, tangible and tactile of crafts.

That's a brilliant metaphor. There's no point in trying to pretend that our world is not increasingly reliant on technology, but that doesn't mean we have lost the ability to create beautiful things that exist in the real world, with just our own two hands, two needles and a length of yarn.

We can dip our toes into both of these worlds, without having to turn our backs on either, and that's a fantastic position to be in.

EQUIPMENT [CH.3]

What stuff do you need, in order to be able to let your inner knitter out? The simple answer is: nothing more than two pointy sticks and some string! Essentially, you can do everything you need to with just these simple tools, and people have been knitting that way for centuries.

My *preferred* answer, however, is a little more involved than that.

The technology and the knowledge base about what goes into how we knit, and how our bodies respond to the process, is actually quite advanced. Consequently, a vast array of different types of equipment has evolved to suit pretty much any need or preference. If you want to be able to use a particular type of wool, on a needle of a particular shape, chances are pretty good that someone out there will be selling it! (And yes, square and triangular knitting needles exist, and can be really beneficial for people living with arthritis that affects their hands.)

I don't want to bamboozle you too much at this fragile, early stage, frightening you off with pages and pages of information that you might not think is relevant at this point in your knitting journey—after all, you haven't even knitted a single stitch yet, so why ever would you need to know about the differences between bamboo and metal needles?

I'll tell you why, and this might surprise you: choosing the right equipment to begin with just might mean the difference between enjoying knitting so much that you never want to stop or hating every second of it, then throwing it in a corner, never to be touched again.

Dramatic?

Well, perhaps a little, but there's truth in it too. Many's the time I've found working on a particular project a total slog and a chore, because I was using a type of yarn that I didn't like or needles that annoyed me.

The whole idea behind knitting is that it has to be fun. It has to be enjoyable. Otherwise, it's just a pretty slow and steady way to turn you into a stressed-out, tightly wound ball of frustrated swearwords.

With practice, and some trial and error, you'll learn what sort of needles you like to use, and what types of fibres you like to knit with. Every knitter is different, with different preferences: perhaps you will be a knitter who only wants to make scarves, or only jumpers, or only socks. Perhaps you'll fall in love with lace, but hate cables, or the other way around.

It's also true that different combinations of needles and yarn are better suited to different projects, so it might be that further down the line, you find that you use one style of needles for socks, and a totally different kind when making a shawl.

But I'm getting ahead of myself. This is only supposed to be an overview, to give you some idea of what is out there. There's so much that I want to share with you, though, it's hard to know where to start.

Straight Needles

KNITTING NEEDLES

We might as well start with knitting needles, as these are the fundamental tools with which you will be working. (And you probably thought that the needles were the only things you'd be learning about in this chapter—this, my friend, is only the tip of the iceberg…)

Knitting needles come in a variety of forms, with a great many variations in each subgroup, but they can mostly be broken down into three main categories: straight needles, circular needles, and double-pointed needles (or DPNs).

STRAIGHT NEEDLES

These are the ones that you will no doubt be most familiar with, from seeing your grandmother using them as she churned out baby cardi after baby cardi with terrifying speed, sparks coming from her fingers. They are the most traditional type of knitting needle around, and are, as the name suggests, long and straight, tapering to a point at the tip, and with some kind of nobble or stopper on the other end to stop your stitches from coming off where they shouldn't.

You can get straight needles in many lengths. If you are only making something small, like a hat made in two pieces, you won't want to have very long needles, as they can be a bit unwieldy and inconvenient to flap about. If you are making something larger, however, like a shawl or a blanket, you'll need to have needles that are long enough to hold however many stitches you are working with.

In the interests of keeping the idea of knitting cool and edgy, it's worth pointing out here that this sort of needle is *definitely* what people most associate with what is often patronisingly called 'nana knitting', but please, don't rule them out! They absolutely have their place in today's kit list, and many male knitters that I know would be lost without them.

Double Pointed Needles [DPNs]

D°UBLE-P°INTED NEEDLES [DPNS]

If you've ever seen someone knitting a sock in the traditional manner and wondered what on earth they could be doing, apart from some monstrous, multi-dimensional cats' cradle with a lot of very pointy things, then they were probably using double-pointed needles.

In simpler times, most garments were knitted in pieces and then sewn together with seams, rather like tailored garments are today. In fact, they very deliberately emulated the tailoring methods of the time—a great deal was already known about the engineering of the structure of clothing, so why try to reinvent the wheel?

There are some people, however, and I include myself among them, who just don't want to make a jumper with separate back and front pieces, which have to be sewn together up the sides. That sounds like far too much hard work.

And what about socks? Who wants to have an uncomfortable seam running up the centre of a sock, causing blisters and unsightly red pressure lines on your skin?

No one, I assure you!

Instead, you want to be able to knit your sock all in one piece, going around and around, never having to stop and turn the work, and never having to break up the smooth, even texture of the fabric with anything as pokey-outy and unsightly as a seam!

What, then, is the answer?

Enter knitting in the round. I'm not going to go into too much detail about that here—there's a whole section of this book devoted to that later—but suffice to say, knitting in the round is a method of knitting in what is actually a continuous spiral, thus completely eliminating the need for seams.

Take a bow, double-pointed needles!

Double-pointed needles, or DPNs, usually come in sets of four or five. It's up to the knitter to decide how many they prefer to use. (Actually, most today come in sets of five. If you prefer using only four, you can keep one as a spare, for when you inevitably lose one…)

As their name suggests, they have a point at each end, so that you can knit your stitches onto one end, and off from the other.

DPNs can be found in a variety of lengths, depending on how much room you require for the number of stitches in your row. They can be anything from four inches to nine inches in length, but standard sizes seem to be either six or eight inches. The sleeves of a jumper might require longer DPNs, but the fingers of a glove might be better on the shortest you can find!

Most of the information you'll find out there on the web will be appropriate to female knitters, who make up the largest sector of the knitting community, so I think it's worth saying that you might find certain lengths really uncomfortable to work with, even though they seem to be perfectly fine for most other people. Working with the wrong length could mean that the points end up rubbing against the palm of your hand. After a while, that can get surprisingly painful. You'll have to try a few for yourself and see what works best with your type of grip and the size of your hand.

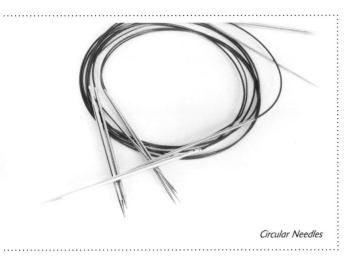

Circular Needles

CIRCULAR NEEDLES

This is a bit of a misnomer. The needle tips on a pair of 'circs', as they are often called, are just as straight as any other needles I've mentioned so far. What makes the needles circular, however, is a length of plasticised cord, or cable, that runs from the back end—or the non-pointy end—of one needle tip to the back end of the other. This cable is flexible, and you can bend it to bring one needle point around to meet the other, essentially creating a circle on which you can work round and round.

Circular needles are a relatively new invention in the knitting canon. Wikipedia tells me that the first US patent for a circular needle was filed in 1918, although they may have been in use in Europe since a little before that. In the short time that they have been around, however, they have totally revolutionised how many people knit today.

Some sets of circs have fixed tips, and you will need to get hold of a different set for each needle size you might need. Alternatively, you can buy sets of circs with detachable tips. These are usually called interchangeable needles, or just 'interchangeables', and you can screw any sized tips that you need to use onto the cables. This gives the knitter greater flexibility about what sizes he can work with, without having to buy hundreds of different sets of needles. It also means you can change the tips during the same project, if you need to switch to smaller or larger needles (and sometimes one does!) with ease.

Admission time: I only ever knit with circs—in fact, I don't even *possess* a pair of straight needles. I very rarely, if ever, use DPNs. I find that all of my knitting needs can be served with an interchangeable set of circs.

It should be stated, in case it wasn't already obvious, that circs are not just used for knitting in the round. You can knit ANY type of knitting using circular needles. Going back to the example of a jumper made from seamed, flat pieces, it's just as easy to knit those pieces using circular needles, rather than straights. There are added benefits to doing so, as well: with circs the weight of the fabric stays on the cable and sits comfortably on your lap. With straights, that weight is carried on the outer ends of the needles and can put a lot of strain and pressure on the wrists and arms of the knitter.

But while we're on the subject of why circs are the terrier's tackle, if you want to talk about knitting in the round with them, rather than with DPNs, here are some of the other benefits of doing so:

* You only need one needle, rather than four or five, and there is no chance of losing one, as the two tips are joined together.

* There is less shifting stuff about, as you don't reach the joins between the needles quite so often. This means that the whole process can feel a lot smoother.

* There is absolutely no chance of your stitches dropping off the back of the needle. This is something that can easily happen when using DPNs.

* If you are knitting on the go, for example on the Tube, as I often do, and you happen to reach your stop sooner than expected, you can simply pull the needle tips out of the work, mid-row or not, thus transferring the stitches onto the cable, where they are perfectly safe. You can then stuff the work in your pocket, or in a bag, without having to worry about them ever sliding loose.

I could go on and on.

Are you starting to sense that I have a rather strong bias here? You'd be right: I definitely do, but I don't want to suggest that what works for me will necessarily be the best option for you. Every knitter has his or her preference for what type of needles to use, and in what situation. You might find that when you knit socks you only want to use DPNs but would rather knit a hat with circs, yet scarves with straight needles. There's absolutely no reason why that shouldn't be the case.

Some people find that using a long, straight needle, anchored under one arm or the other, gives them more control over their work, and therefore they can get up a greater speed.

On the other hand, some people find that style of knitting is just too cumbersome and it slows them down, rather than speeds them up.

What matters most is that you find the type of needle that is most comfortable for *you*, for *this* piece of knitting. Comfort and ease are vital for a long and happy knitting life. After all, you'll be making the same tiny movements over and over again, many hundreds of thousands of times over the years, and you want that process to be something that brings you joy and peace of mind, rather than a repetitive strain injury!

Nathan's Needle Bag

NEEDLE MATERIALS

All of the above types of needle can be made from a variety of different materials: metal, plastic, wood, bamboo, carbon fibre, etc. All have different properties, and you'll find the ones you like best with a bit of trial and error.

Some materials are slicker than others, and many beginners find that metal needles, for example, might be too slippery for when they are just starting out. Wood, or bamboo, grips the yarn a little bit more and can stop your stitches from sliding off the ends so easily.

I use metal tips for everything. I like the speed.

Avoid plastic. It squeaks.

Interchangeable Needle Set

NEEDLE SIZE

Knitting needles come in a whole range of sizes. This time, I'm not talking about the length of the needle, but rather its thickness or diameter.

The size of the needle dictates the size of the stitch. Think about it: it only takes a tiny amount of yarn to wrap around the circumference of a needle that is only 2mm in diameter. It will take much more yarn to wrap around a needle that measures 8mm across, and stitch size is dictated by, among other things, the amount of yarn that is used to create that individual stitch. That's logic, that is!

STUFF TO KNOW

My GCSE maths tells me that because circumference = diameter x pi, it will take 6.28mm of yarn to go around a 2mm needle, and 25.13mm of yarn to go around an 8mm needle.

That's a huge difference and will obviously make a MUCH larger stitch.

Did you think you could buy one set of knitting needles, and that they would do for everything you might ever want to knit? Oh my good fellow, no. Sorry about that.

When I first started knitting, I genuinely thought that once I owned a pair of knitting needles, I was all set. I quickly learnt that's just not the case. You will need needles in a great variety of different sizes, and if you're anything like me, tending to have more than one project on the go at any one time, the likelihood is that you will need duplicate sets in the sizes you use most often.

Depending on where you are in the world, needle sizes are labelled in different ways. Here in the UK, the modern way is to label the needles by diameter, measured in millimetres. To me, this is the most sensible way to make sure that you get a standard size needle, as a millimetre in one part of the world is the same as a millimetre anywhere else! Sadly, although I think the knitting world *is* catching on to the sense of this, it is happening very slowly, and there are a number of other sizing scales still in use.

Older UK needles have a number on them which tells you the size, but it's not linked to a measurement that would make a great deal of sense to our brains these days.

STUFF TO KNOW

Old UK needle sizes are taken from the traditional method of measuring wire gauge, which is something to do with how many times a metal rod was passed through a 'draw plate' to stretch it and to thin it. The more times it had been drawn (i.e. the higher the number), the thinner it would become.

To my 21st-century mind, labelling something in this way sounds a little ridiculous, but there are still a great many needles knocking around out there that are numbered thus. They are still perfectly fit for purpose and have possibly been handed down from generation to generation, making them highly treasured items.

Because so many still exist, it's important to know about this sizing system in order to make sure that you are using the appropriately sized needles for the project that you are working on.

In the US, they do things differently. Just like formatting their dates... With the older British system, the higher the number, the smaller the needle. With the US system, still very much in place today, the exact opposite is true. Why would anything be straightforward...?

As the needles get smaller, so do the numbers used to name them. I have absolutely no idea what these numbers might originally have been based on. For all I know, they might be entirely arbitrary! Do be warned, however: if you are using an old pair of British needles, and the pattern you are working on is written by an American designer, you could get into a proper pickle! A British size 1 needle, for example, is 7.5mm. That's a pretty big needle. In the US system, a size 1 needle is 2.25mm. A world of difference! (Oddly, you'd be fine if the pattern requires a 4.5mm needle, as that is the only size where the old UK and US systems agree. For interest, they both call it a size 7!)

Standard sizes range from 2mm at the lower end up to 10mm or 12mm for larger needles, but it's perfectly possible to find needles much smaller or larger than this, if you happen to need them.

See the following chart for comparison.

METRIC SIZES	OLD UK SIZES	US SIZES
2.0mm	14	0
2.25mm	13	1
2.5mm	-	1.5
2.75mm	12	2
3.0mm	11	-
3.25mm	10	3
3.5mm	-	4
3.75mm	9	5
4.0mm	8	6*
4.5mm	7	7
5.0mm	6	8
5.5mm	5	9
6.0mm	4	10
6.5mm	3	10.5
7.0mm	2	-
7.5mm	1	-
8.0mm	0	11
9.0mm	00	13
10.0mm	000	15
12.0mm	-	17

Sometimes listed as 4.25mm

Project Bags

°THER USEFUL EQUIPMENT

PR°JECT BAG

Any piece of knitting you are currently working on is called a 'project'. Project bags come in a range of shapes, sizes, and fabrics. Small ones are great for socks, but you'll want something much larger for a jumper. Yeah, you can certainly stuff your knitting in the bottom of your rucksack, or in a deep pocket, but the project bag will protect your work from dirt and fluff and stop it snagging on sharp things.

It's useful for holding not just the actual knitting, but also the pattern you might be working from, along with any notions (see below) you might require. Having a specific bag to hold everything you might need while working on a particular project is a really good way of keeping things organised. You can just grab it and go, knowing it's all in there. Of course, your project bag might just be a supermarket placky bag. No harm in that, but a sturdy cloth bag will probably do a better job and be less prone to tearing.

Because I often have more than one project on the go at any one time, I find having unique project bags helps me find whichever project I might be looking for at any given time.

N°TI°NS

Apart from the yarn itself, there are lots of other little accoutrements that go along with knitting to make your life easier. They are often collectively known as 'notions'.

Funny little word, isn't it: notions? Apart from the sense of being 'a fanciful, or whimsical idea', in North America it seems the word is associated with sewing equipment, like pins and buttons, etc. That sense has been adopted by the knitting world. Sources on the web all describe its usage in this context as being specifically American, but I can assure you it is now very common parlance over here in the UK too. (Rather strangely, it is always used in the plural. You won't ever hear someone referring to a stitch marker as 'a notion'.)

When I first started knitting, I remember saying to myself, 'Why would I ever need to buy any of that stuff? I can get by perfectly well using everyday objects that I already have.' You will no doubt think exactly the same thing at first, but I predict it won't be long before you start building up your own little collection of 'other stuff'. You'll soon find lots of little bits and pieces that make your knitting life run that little bit more smoothly, or more conveniently, and that's never a bad thing!

Notions Bag

Looking in my own notions bag right now, I'll go through the things I have gathered along the way and share why they are useful. You can make up your own mind as to whether you think they are must-have-can't-live-without items or simply too-much-clutter-take-them-away items.

TAPE MEASURE

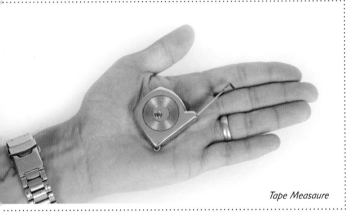

Tape Measure

Probably the most important thing in my notions bag, my tape measure is only tiny—about a metre in length—but I turn to it surprisingly frequently. If you are making *anything* that requires the finished object to be a particular size—which will be most of the time—then you will always want to have a tape measure to hand. That way, you can check every so often to see if you've reached the right length or the right width.

Listen, you don't need me to tell you how to use a tape measure, but believe me, you'll find it way more useful than you ever thought possible. Ignore this advice if you choose, but if you are approaching a critical stage in your knitting, and you don't have one to hand…

NEEDLE GAUGE

A needle gauge is usually a flat piece of metal, plastic or wood with little notches or holes cut into it. Each notch/hole is a different size and relates to the diameter of a knitting needle. They come in a wide variety of shapes.

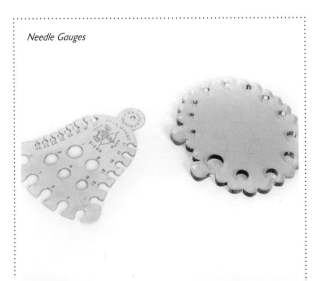

Needle Gauges

With a gauge that has side notches, instead of putting the *tip* of your needle through the hole by the notch, you have to put the *side* of your needle into the notch itself.

Bell Gauge with Side Notches

Newer ones, like the blue plastic sheep in the pic, will have metric sizes on them, and holes drilled through the centre of the surface. It's much more obvious how to use them.

Bell Gauge with Side Notches

Although most needles you can buy will be labelled with their size, you'll often find that the label can come off, or wear away. While it's true that you'll get better at recognising different sizes by eye to a certain degree, needle size is such an important factor in getting knitted things to fit, so you'd be wise to have access to a needle gauge. I don't use mine very often, but it has definitely come in handy on the odd occasion!

Stitch Markers

STITCH MARKERS

Stitch markers are very useful for reminding you where you are in your knitting. If you are working on a project that features a stitch pattern that repeats say, every 24 stitches, you might want to place stitch markers in your work at 24-stitch intervals. That way, you can see at a glance where the next repeat should begin, and it can help you to keep track of what you are supposed to be doing.

Some patterns will specify where you should place a marker, and you will see instructions that say something like, 'Knit to 2 stitches before marker, then knit two stitches together'. In this case, the marker is a vital part of the process, as it ensures that you will do all the right things in all the right places.

Stitch Marker In Situ

A stitch marker only has to be something that you can slip over the tip of your knitting needle, between two stitches. On every row, when you get to the marker, you simply slide it from one needle to the other, and helpfully, it will always be there on the row that you are currently knitting.

You can get stitch markers with loads of things dangling from them. Often, the things that dangle simply get in the way or have pointy corners that snag in your yarn. Amusing is all very well, but make sure you are using something that is fit for purpose.

You don't need anything fancy. When I first started knitting, I made my own stitch markers out of a little loop of yarn in a colour that showed up well against the yarn I was knitting with. I tied a knot in it, so the loop was just large enough to fit over my needle, and off I went. It works perfectly well.

Yarn Stitch Marker

To be honest, I like my markers to be as plain as possible, so a little metal ring on its own is just perfect for me, but there is also something to be said for having markers that look noticeably different from each other, as you might want to use one to denote the start of a round, one to show you where the start of a particular section of stitch patterning begins, and others for each repeat of the pattern, so being able to tell one from the other can be very useful.

Yarn Stitch Marker In Situ

PRºGRESS KEEPERS

A progress keeper can often look very much like a stitch marker. The key difference is that instead of having a closed metal ring, it will have a little lobster-claw clip, or some other opening fastener.

You clip the progress keeper directly onto the fabric of the knitting, rather than slipping it onto one of your needles. This means that instead of travelling up the work with you, a progress keeper stays exactly where you put it. This can be useful if you need to know that you started a new section of the pattern at a certain point, and you need to work a certain number of rows of the new section before moving on. Clip your progress keeper to the first row of the new section, and you don't have to count all the rows that went before it.

If you are counting rows on a project that is very long indeed, you can add progress keepers at regular intervals. That way, if you lose count, you only have to go back to the last progress keeper, instead of having to go all the way back to the beginning. First world problems, I know, but losing your place can be incredibly frustrating, and counting large numbers of something tiny can be really hard!

You might simply want to place a keeper at the beginning of the day, so that you can see how much you have knitted before calling it a night. On a slow-moving project, it can sometimes be quite demoralising if you don't get to see it getting noticeably larger. Popping in a progress keeper at the start of the session can give you a sense of tangible achievement, and the motivation to keep going tomorrow.

Trust me: it's a thing.

Progress Keepers In Situ

Darning/Tapestry Needles

DARNING NEEDLE/TAPESTRY NEEDLE

These needles are a very important part of your knitting arsenal. When you finish knitting a project, you will find that you have lots of tails of yarn (called simply 'ends') hanging off your work. If you have knitted something simple, you'll probably only have two ends to deal with—one where you started, and one where you finished—but if you used multiple colours, or your yarn broke, or you used more than one ball of yarn on a larger project, you might end up with quite a few.

To make everything look neat and tidy, you'll want to hide those ends, and you can do this by weaving them into the fabric of the piece. If you simply cut them off close to the fabric so that they don't show, the knitting will start to unravel, and large holes will appear. That's *not* what you want at all!

Darning needles are brilliant for this job, as they usually have a nice large eye, making it easier to get thicker yarn through, and they are typically quite blunt, which makes the job a lot less frustrating: a sharper sewing needle will split the yarn all too easily, and make it much more difficult for you to put it where you want it.

Yarn Cutter

YARN CUTTER

This is exactly what it sounds like. Something that cuts your yarn. Yes, you're a strong chap, and yes, you can most probably snap it using sheer brute strength, but be warned: some yarns are stronger than they appear, and my misplaced faith in my ability to snap certain yarns by hand has left me with friction burns and cuts on many occasions! You can never be quite sure

where the yarn will break, and it leaves a very messy end to your yarn tail, making things trickier later on when it comes to threading that tail onto your tapestry needle.

My own yarn cutter has no exposed blade, and instead has little notches around its sides. You pass the yarn through these notches where they make contact with a little hidden blade, tucked safely inside. The yarn gets cut neatly and accurately, exactly how and where you want it. Yes, it's true that a small pair of scissors will do the job perfectly well, but I often knit on planes, and carrying scissors in your hand luggage is asking for trouble. (Ask me how I know…)

R°W COUNTER

Row Counters

Row counters are useful, just as long as you have the kind of brain that will remember to use them properly. (Sadly, I don't have that kind of brain so I rarely use mine, but it comes in useful every now and then.)

Essentially, a yarn counter is a little device that displays numbers on it. Some have click buttons to change the number from one to two, from two to three, and so on, and some have a wheel that you have to manually spin, but they all do the same job.

Click Counter

Starting at zero, you add one at the end of each row you complete. As long as you are diligent about it, you don't have to keep count in your head of how many rows you have worked.

Keeping track of how many rows you have knitted is important for a couple of reasons. Firstly, if you are following a pattern, it's important to know which row of the pattern you are on at any point. Secondly, you might be instructed to knit a certain number of rows before moving on to the next section. It can be quite difficult to count the rows of certain types of knitting, so staying abreast of where you are, as you go along, is much simpler.

Twist Counter

I know what you're saying: it's only counting. I'm sure I can remember what row I'm on. And you might be right. But what happens when you get distracted, or when you get sleepy, or you get so tired that you have to put the knitting away and don't have time to pick it up again for a few days/weeks/years*? (*Delete as applicable: only you know how busy your life is!) Are you quite so confident that after all that time, you'll still remember how many rows of knitting you had done? I'm not so sure. Anything that makes it easier to see where you have reached in your knitting is a very good thing in my book. And for the record, this actually *is* my book!

CABLE NEEDLE

Cable needles are used when knitting a pattern that looks like the columns of stitches twist over and round each other, a bit like a piece of rope. Think old knitted fishermen's jumpers, or a traditional Aran jumper.

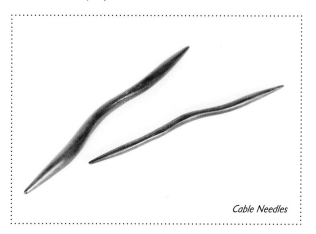

Cable Needles

A cable needle is a short needle (ideally the same diameter as the needles you are working with), designed to help make cabling easier.

Cable needles are a bit like very short DPNs, tapered to a point at both ends. They can be entirely straight, or have a curved bump in the middle, or they might be folded back on themselves, rather like a capital letter 'U'.

TIP

It's perfectly possible to do most types of cable without using a cable needle, but while you are learning about this stuff, it's much better to use one. The techniques in this book advocate the use of a cable needle, but if you want to do some homework on cabling without, YouTube is a great resource for tutorials.

SMALL CROCHET HOOK

Hang on: a crochet hook? Isn't this a KNITTING manual? I didn't sign up for crochet—that's a step TOO far…!

Cool your jets, my friend. The little crochet hook I always carry around in my knitting bag is one of the most useful items I possess. Fact. Full stop. Exclamation mark. And I don't ever use it for crochet!

Small Crochet Hook

Knitting is a succession of loops pulled through other loops, and sometimes, those loops can slip off your needle. With nothing to hold them in place, a whole lot of unravelling can occur, and before you know it, you're in a proper tangle.

Once you know a little bit about the structure of the knitted fabric, however, your friendly crochet hook can save your life. Well, if not your life, then at least your knitting.

Using the hook, you can grab hold of errant loops of yarn, so much more easily than with stubby, blokey fingers and thumbs. Once you've got it on the end of your hook, it's as easy as pie to manipulate that recalcitrant strand of yarn and get it back where you want it before it can run off any further. The amount of time and effort—and swearing—I have saved by being able to do a quick fix with a crochet hook is immeasurable. Get a crochet hook. You'll thank me later.

SENSITIVE SCALES

I use my scales a LOT. Ideally you want scales that are sensitive to a tenth of a gram. Weighing your yarn tells you how much you have. Knowing how much you have can mean the difference between having enough, and not being able to finish something. You can make all sorts of decisions based on knowing how much yarn you have.

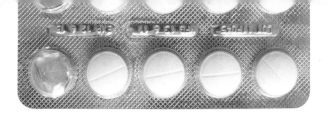

HEADACHE TABLETS (SERIOUSLY, DUDE!)

You think I'm joking? I kid you not. There's nothing worse than sitting down for a nice couple of hours of knitting time, and finding a headache coming on. There's a lot of brainwork involved in knitting: working your brain that hard when it's in the throes of a headache can be punishing beyond measure!

Do yourself a favour and make sure you always have some headache tablets to hand. You'll never regret having them there, but I guarantee you'd regret it if they weren't!

WATER

Keep hydrated.

Knitting requires a lot of concentration, and often involves long periods of sitting still. It can be easy to forget to drink for hours on end, and one of the first things to suffer when the brain gets dehydrated is cognitive processing. Be kind to yourself, and to your knitting: always have water nearby.

IN SUMMARY

There are hundreds of other things that you could add to your collection, but to my mind, these are the main ones that you are likely to need or find a use for. You can spend as little or as much on them as you like: there's a massive range of products out there and a huge market for them as well.

I tend not to go for anything too fussy or overly complex. That's my male brain at work. I'm not really a fluffy sort of guy. As long as it does the job, that's good enough for me, but you might like the idea of getting a set of stitch markers that look like mini tools from your tool kit, or like your favourite Disney princesses, or like Liquorice Allsorts.

You certainly don't need to go out right away, armed with a massive shopping list, just because I have said that I find these things useful. I'd suggest waiting to see how you get on without. Just get hold of what you need, as and when you need it.

The good news is, the choice is yours.

AN INTRODUCTION TO YARN [CH.4]

Hmm… this is a tricky one! There's an enormous amount to know about yarn, and if you're anything like me, the more you learn: the more you'll *want* to learn. How much of it is really relevant though, to someone just starting out?

None of this knowledge is really essential right now, but it rather goes back to what I was saying earlier about the right equipment being a factor in helping you to decide whether you enjoy knitting or not. Knowing a bit about what types of yarn are suitable for what types of project can be really useful. You might find out, right off the bat, that there are some fibres you really *hate* working with. If you choose one of those detested fibres for your first project, you might never want to knit again.

That would make me sad.

In that case, let's go a for a basic overview, and if it's something you want to know more about, you can go off and do as much further reading as you like. That's what our mutual friend the Internet is for!

You'll have noticed that I've used the word 'yarn' here, rather than the word 'wool'. You may not have thought about it before, but there's a difference. Wool refers specifically to the fibre that comes from a sheep, but you can knit with many different types of fibres from many different sources. So while it's true to say that all wool is yarn, it's most certainly not true to say that all yarn is wool.

But what's all the fuss about? Regardless of what you choose to call it, yarn is yarn, right?

Wrong!

Different fibres, and the yarns made with them, have different properties that make them more or less suitable for different projects. You can also blend different fibres together, combining a desirable property from one fibre with a different desirable property from another.

TYPES ºF FIBRE

MAN-MADE FIBRES

Most people start off knitting with man-made fibres. I do wish they wouldn't. Acrylic is the most common non-natural fibre used for making yarn and is the go-to material for a lot of new knitters, mainly because it is incredibly inexpensive. I totally understand this: after all, why would you spend loads of money on the luxury fibres out there, when you don't even know if you enjoy the process of knitting yet? The answer is simple: you'll enjoy knitting with a natural fibre a lot more.

It's certainly true that there are many brands of acrylic yarn out there, some of which will be blended with a small amount of actual wool, in order to feel a bit more realistic, and they can be wonderfully soft to the touch once knitted up. It's also usually machine washable, which makes it the ideal material for knitting anything for babies, as we all know what mess factories babies can be!

There are other types of man-made fibre that you will find in knitting yarn as well. Nylon, for example, is often to be found in yarn that is used for knitting socks. It's a good idea to have a blend of perhaps 80% natural fibres with 20% nylon when knitting socks. Of all knitted items, socks probably get the most wear and tear, and after spending all that time working on your wonderful hand-knit socks, the last thing you want is for them to go through at the toe or the heel after about three wears! Oh, and you can help that, by the way, by cutting your toenails more regularly! Don't think I don't know…

The environmentalist in me feels obliged to point out that acrylic fibres are partially to blame for the profusion of microplastics that are finding their way into our rivers, oceans, and ultimately, our food chain. If you are keen not to add to this very real problem, then natural fibres are the way forward.

ANIMAL FIBRES

The most well-known animal fibre for use in producing fibre will be that of the sheep. There you are, we can now actually talk about wool, and not worry about looking foolish in front of people in the know!

It's not that simple, though (of course it's not!), as there are literally hundreds of varieties of sheep, and their fleeces all have very different properties, leading to the creation of very different types of wool.

The softness of the wool is governed by two main things. (Spinners will tell you that there are many more variables than this, but I'm trying to keep this simple, people!) Those two things are the thickness of the individual fibre (referred to as the micron count) and the overall length of each fibre (known as the staple length). The finer and longer the fibre, the softer and more luxurious the yarn will be. Conversely, the shorter and thicker the fibres, the coarser and scratchier it will feel. Other factors do come into play, of course, such as whether or not the fibre is straight or crinkly, but thickness and length—as so often—are the main factors here…

Merino is one of the softest sheep wools available, with a micron count of around 12–13 microns at the finer end, making it perfect for scarves or anything worn next to the skin. It's less suitable for making socks with, unless blended with some percentage of nylon, because being so soft it can wear through in no time at all.

Bluefaced Leicester (BFL) is fast becoming one of the most popular fibres in the knitting world. It is soft—almost like merino—but has a spring to it and a dense structure that makes it ideal for maintaining really good stitch definition in your work. It's perfect for cables and other visual textures, and has a silklike sheen to the way it reflects light. It is significantly harder-wearing than merino, and is one of my favourite fibres to work with. (If you are reading this in the US, 'Leicester' is pronounced 'Lester'. Additionally, this is true of London's 'Leicester Square', so I've also just helped to stop you getting laughed at by locals on the tube for saying, "How many stops to Lye-chester Square?")

Shetland wool comes in a variety of natural shades: creams, greys, and beige through to darker browns and almost black. It's a much coarser fibre than either merino or BFL, with a micron count of about 28–33, making it by no means the crunchiest fibre out there, but before you write it off, it has some other amazing properties. If you are making a traditional Fair Isle jumper, you want to have a wool that 'grips' onto itself so that the fabric doesn't come apart. Shetland wool is perfect for this and makes the job of knitting with it much easier than with a smoother, finer yarn. It is also incredibly durable, and your jumper will last for many years.

There's Gotland, Polwarth, Zwartbles, Wensleydale, and the universe alone knows how many others. And they are all different. And suitable for different things. A sheep is certainly not just a sheep when it comes to its fleece.

Let's not forget alpaca, llama, camel, goat (cashmere and mohair), yak, musk ox (qiviut), rabbit (angora), vicuña (a type of camelid), silk, and so many more. They all make wonderful yarns, varying in feel, strength, and colour, as well as suitability for different projects. I'm going to stop there though, as it can get bewildering, and I don't want to drown you in too much information.

PLANT-BASED NATURAL FIBRES

It's not just animal fibres that can be used for making yarn. Cotton, linen, bamboo: these are just some of the plant-based fibres that make wonderful yarns for knitting with. (That's right, you heard: bamboo! You can knit with bamboo yarn on bamboo needles!)

Plant-based fibres tend to be cooler to wear—and to work with—than their animal counterparts, and for people who live in hot climates but still want to knit, cotton particularly can be a great option. It has a lot less give in it than most animal fibres, and that can make it quite tiring for the hands to work with, but I rather think that's a small price to pay.

FIBRE: SUMMING UP

Ultimately, although there will be certain types of yarn that are *better* suited to certain projects than others, it's not something that you really need to bother yourself with at this stage. It's useful to know, however, that there is loads more to learn about this stuff, depending on how deeply you want to delve into it, further down the line.

It's all about giving yourself the best opportunity to fall in love with what you are doing. If you are using equipment that doesn't give you the best experience, you'll never know if it's the right pastime for you or not.

When learning something new, there can be a tendency for new knitters to get a little bit (or sometimes a lot) of tension in their shoulders. That might be because of fear of messing up, or intense concentration, or a combination of the two. This tension can easily make your knitting really tight. Another pitfall for the new knitter to be aware of, is that this tension can also give rise to slightly sweaty hands. Gross. (Don't worry, this stage will pass, the more you get used to what you are doing, I promise.)

The combination of tight stitches and moisture from sweaty hands, however, can make things a bit uncomfortable. The nature of the acrylic fibre is that it isn't at all absorbent, and in no time at all, you can find that your cheap plastic needles actually squeak as you try to insert them into the stitches. Also, as there is no natural give to the yarn, everything keeps on getting tighter and tighter, you have to work harder and harder, your tension levels go through the roof and it all starts to spiral out of control. Headaches, shoulder pain, teeth grinding, stress—not exactly the peaceful, meditative experience that knitting is supposed to be.

Conversely, if you are knitting with a luxury fibre that runs through your hands like melted chocolate, and with well-crafted, metal needles that facilitate the passage of the yarn like high-class oil on well-maintained gears, you'll find that everything flows with grace and ease, and you will actually feel your natural stress and tensions ebbing away. Which of those two experiences is more likely to work for you?

My advice? Get guidance from someone in the know—you probably already know a knitter or two—or talk to the owner of your local yarn shop (LYS) and ask what natural fibres they think would be good for a beginner, based on what you want to make. They'll probably be so delighted that a guy has walked into the shop, they'll be bending over backwards to help you.

In short, give yourself the best shot at making a go of this by getting decent stuff to work with. It doesn't have to be top of the range, but it shouldn't be bottom of the bargain barrel either. That initial investment will pay for itself in 'hours enjoyed while knitting', over and over and over.

YARN WEIGHT

Yarn comes in many different thicknesses. The thickness of a yarn is usually referred to as its 'weight'.

You can get incredibly fine, thin yarn for working diaphanous lace shawls and the like, and you can get really thick and chunky yarn for blankets and bedspreads, or even hammocks or rugs.

Irritatingly, the different categories of yarn weight seem to have lots of different names. Aran-weight yarn in one country might be called worsted-weight yarn in another. And, incidentally, it is!

Here is a very rough table of the different yarn weights and the kind of metreage one can expect to get from them.

Cobweb	900–1100 m/100g
Lace	600–900 m/100g
Fingering/4-ply/Sock	350–500 m/100g
Sport (mostly US)	260–350 m/100g
DK (stands for 'double knitting')	200-260 m/100g
Aran (UK) or Worsted (US)	120–200 m/100g
Chunky (UK) or Bulky (US)	80–120 m/100g
Super Chunky (UK) or Super Bulky (US)	30–80 m/100g

Golly, even as I was putting this chart together, I realised how much crossover there is, and how many discrepancies there are when it comes to labelling yarn weights. It can be infuriating. Some knitters will argue strongly that a certain yarn *can't possibly* be Aran weight, it *must* be a chunky. It sort of doesn't matter! What matters far more is having an accurate way to compare the thickness of one yarn with the thickness of another. That way you can be sure that the yarn you use will have a similar outcome to the yarn used by the designer.

In order to find a suitable yarn for a project, the best thing to do is look at the metreage per 100g. Most yarns will state this on the ball band or label. If you are making a project where the pattern specifies that the yarn used was 400m per 100g (regardless of whether it calls it a sport, a fingering, a 4-ply, a 3-ply, or any of the many other ultimately useless labels), find another yarn that is also 400m per 100g, and you'll be absolutely fine!

And what if the yarn you want to use is slightly different from the one specified in the pattern? Two options:

- Don't be a stubborn arse! Find a different yarn that is the same thickness and save yourself a whole world of pain.

- Make a 'gauge swatch' with different sized needles (see below). If the yarn you want to use has a shorter length per 100g (i.e. 360m/100g instead of 400m/100g), this means that the yarn is slightly thicker than the one used in the pattern. You probably can achieve the required gauge, but you might need to use a slightly smaller needle. Conversely, if the yarn is running longer, say 420m/100g rather than 400m/100g, it means it's slightly thinner, and you may need to go up a needle size or two.

MAKING A GAUGE SWATCH

Making a what? Sometimes also called a tension square, a swatch is just a small piece of knitting, worked in the stitch pattern you will be using for your actual project. It's a little practice piece to let you know that what you will be doing in your actual project is heading in the right direction. Swatches

are important because it's really vital to get the right 'gauge' in your knitting.

Regardless of whether or not your yarn matches the one in the pattern exactly, if you are making something where the fit of the finished object is important (a jumper or cardigan, rather than a scarf), the best advice I can give is to make a gauge swatch anyway. Your knitting tension is quite likely to be different from the designer's, so even with the same yarn and needles, you may end up getting a different number of stitches per inch, just because you are a different person. A gauge swatch will set you on the right path, and tell you if you need to use different needles or even switch to a thicker or thinner yarn.

Gauge Swatch

THE IMPORTANCE OF GAUGE

It's not just important, it's *crucial*. If you're knitting a pattern for a jumper and you want the jumper to fit correctly, you'll need to know not just how many stitches there should be in order to fit around your chest, but also *how big* those stitches need to be.

Every knitter has their own way of knitting. Some people are quite loose knitters and their stitches will be quite large. Other people (me included) are tighter knitters, and create smaller stitches, even if they use the same needles and yarn. That means a piece of knitting 30 stitches across will be wider for the looser knitter than for the tighter one. Even the smallest variation in gauge can add up to make quite a difference when working on a large number of stitches like in a jumper.

If your pattern tells you the recommended gauge is supposed to be 26 sts per 10cm (4in), that means that the ideal situation is to have your own 26 stitches take up 10cm (4in) of fabric.

Follow?

Unlike me, you might be a knitter of looser fabric, and your gauge might be something like 25 sts per 10cm (4in). You think

to yourself, 'close enough: those stitches are only small, so I'll get knitting'.
(I've honestly done this, and believe me, it's never worth it!)

That difference of just one stitch per 10cm (4in) could mean a size discrepancy of 5cm (2in) over the body of a jumper. Those little differences really add up!

It's useful to know that if your gauge is *looser* than that recommended, you will have *fewer* stitches per inch than the stated gauge, as your stitches will be bigger. Conversely, it follows that if you are a *tighter* knitter, you will have *more* stitches per inch, as your stitches will be smaller. (That's often the opposite of what feels intuitive to a lot of people.)

NB: In order to alter your gauge to match the one recommended in the pattern, you *can* decide to use thinner or thicker yarn, but the most consistent way to change your gauge is to use different-sized needles from those specified in the pattern or on the ball band of the yarn. Larger needles give a looser gauge (fewer stitches per inch) and smaller needles give a tighter gauge (more stitches per inch).

H°W T°S [CH.5]

Fanfare at the ready: this is the bit you've been waiting for. You picked this book up, either because you wanted to learn how to knit, or because your boyfriend/girlfriend/husband/wife/significant other thought it was a good idea on your behalf. I'm well aware that we're already on page 38*, and there's not been a whiff of a tutorial yet.

That's actually very deliberate. There are millions of knitting books out there for beginners, and they all give you pretty much the same instructions that I am about to give you. When I set about writing *this* book, however, I had to think long and hard about what I wanted to include. What will make *this* book different from all the others? Is it the fact that it is aimed at men? And what does that *mean*? What *makes* it a book aimed at men? It's certainly not enough to stick a devastatingly handsome guy (me) on the front cover and leave it at that! Oh no. I *could* have just given you the basic moves and started you off with the simplest stitches, taught in the simplest of ways, but that would be just like any other knitting book, and that's just not good enough. Not for me, at any rate and not, dear reader, for you. You deserve more.

I started, then, to realise how much stuff I've learnt and/or worked out and/or picked up along the way. Hundreds of tiny things that make my knitting life easier now than it was when I first started. That knowledge base informs every decision I make about my knitting, and it occurred to me that if I had known everything I know about knitting now, back then, perhaps it would have been easier for me to go further, sooner.

And so here we are. This is *my* book, taught in *my* way. It's the way *I* would've wanted to have been taught, if I had known then what I now know I needed to know, before I had known I needed to know it.

Ridiculous sentence. Anyway…

This is the section of the book where you will really start to get to grips with the mechanics of knitting. Don't worry if it all feels a bit awkward at first: that's totally normal. This stuff is new to you, and you'll be using your hands in ways they aren't used to working.

I've got good news for you: recent research studies have shown that we create memories by reinforcing neural pathways in our brains. Repeatedly thinking the same thoughts, or making the same movements over and over, actually changes the topography of our brains, and creates new neural pathways that simply didn't exist before. It is in these new pathways that we lay down our memories.

The movements you make when you knit are movements that you will be repeating over and over, many times in succession, and it won't be long before what we have always called muscle memory kicks in. It's not really *muscle* memory: it's *neural* memory, and you will be walking the same pathways in your brain, again and again, making it easier to access those well-trodden memories, to the point where it feels like your muscles are doing it all by themselves.

Before you know it, your hands will find their own way of working: the way that works just right for you. And that's science!

We've discussed the different sizes of needles and the different thicknesses of yarn, and why it's important to use a yarn/needle combo that works for the type of fabric you want to create. For all of the tutorials in this How-To section, it's a good idea to use nice thick wool and needles that match. I recommend some DK-weight yarn and a pair of 4mm needles, or thereabouts. Enough theory: let's do something practical, and actually get some loops on your needles!

*I know there aren't any page numbers in this little area of the book—that's because the pics are too nice—but don't worry, I've worked it out, and trust me: it's page 38.

TYING A SLIP KNOT

The first of those loops is the humble slip knot. It's a basic step that you will need to familiarise yourself with, as it's one that you will use an awful lot.

Some knitters hate having knots in their work, asserting that you can feel them in the texture of the fabric. I'm sure that's true, if you REALLY try hard to feel for them, but it doesn't bother me. Who goes around pinching someone else's knitting, just to see if there are any invisible knots in it?

Rude!

(In fairness, I sometimes do...)

A knot can be the difference between your work staying together, or unravelling before your eyes, and I know which I'd prefer. As far as I'm concerned, it's best to err on the side of caution.

The joy of a slip knot, of course, is that you get the stability of the knot itself, but you can always undo it later if your knot-o-phobia strikes at any point!

Most of you will already know how to do this, and the following steps are only one way of many that exist. Feel free to ignore this section if tying a slip knot is already in your skill base!

**I've recorded a shedload of videos to accompany all of the tutorials in this book.
If you have a QR code reader on your phone, zap the codes to visit each vid.**

SCAN TO WATCH
MY 'TYING A SLIP KNOT' VID

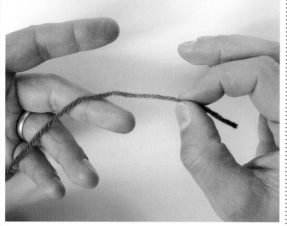

STEP 1

Hold your yarn so that the bit that leads to the end (known as the tail) is pointing towards the right, and the bit that leads to the ball (called the working yarn) is pointing towards your left.

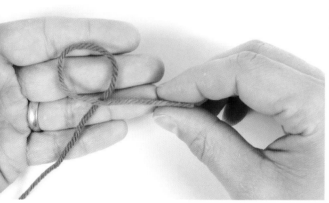

STEP 2

Holding the tail end in your right hand and the other end in your left, make a loop of yarn so that the tail-end yarn crosses over in front of the ball-end yarn.

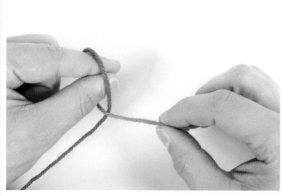

STEP 3

With your left thumb and forefinger, reach through the loop, going in from the top.

STEP 4

With your left thumb and forefinger, grab the yarn that leads to the tail. (Don't let go of the end of the tail with your right hand.)

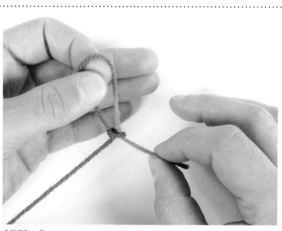

STEP 5

Using your left thumb and forefinger, pull a new loop through the original loop.

STEP 6

Pull on the end that leads to the ball to tighten the knot—don't overtighten—and now you have a loop that you can make larger or smaller at will. It only needs to be big enough to fit over your knitting needle. Hey presto!

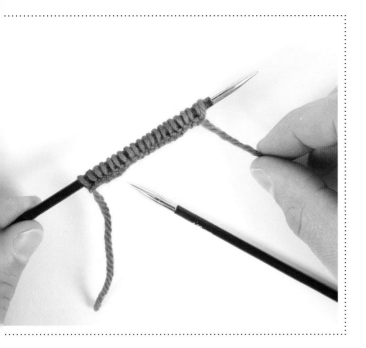

CASTING °N

Knitting is just a series of loops, through which you pull another series of loops. There's not much more to it than that. To start with, you need to learn a way of creating that very first row of loops, and they, in turn, will form the foundation for the rest of your knitting.

Making that first row of loops is called 'casting on', and there are dozens, if not hundreds, of different ways of doing it. Some ways are more complicated than others, some are more decorative, or stretchier than others. Some suit certain situations better than others. We're not going to worry about all of that for now. You are going to learn what most people refer to as the 'knitted-on cast on', although most people wouldn't bother to add the hyphen, even though they should, as the two words, 'knitted', and, 'on', in this instance, are forming a phrasal adjective, but that's an argument for another time…

The knitted-on cast on is one of the simplest of methods of casting on stitches, and a really good place to start when learning to knit. Once you are holding the needles and yarn correctly, it has just four basic steps, and once you get to grips with them, you'll be able to cast on any project you like with ease. You might never *need* to learn another type of cast on, as this one will work in most situations.

NB: It might be worth knowing that all of the patterns in this book use this type of cast on.

That's no accident, by the way…

KNITTING STYLES

From this point onwards, you'll mostly be holding two knitting needles, one in each hand, and manipulating your yarn at the same time. It might be worth pausing here, therefore, to have a chat about knitting styles.

I'm sure you're already sick and tired of hearing me say this, but knitting doesn't ever seem to have just one way of doing anything. In fact, I would probably go as far as to say that there are as many different ways to knit as there are knitters! People even *hold* their knitting in different ways, and it can be hard to imagine how someone else's way of doing things could possibly work, but for *them*, it does.

Some knitters hold their yarn in their left hand. This is often called 'Continental knitting'. The yarn wraps over the left forefinger, and the knitter uses the needle in the right hand to pick at the yarn in order to make the stitch. As a result, these knitters are sometimes called 'pickers'.

Continental Knitting

On the other hand (pun absolutely intended!), some knitters hold their yarn in their right hand. This method is commonly referred to as the 'English' style. Among English-style knitters, you have 'throwers', who move their right hand backwards and forwards to wrap the yarn around the needle and 'flickers'.

English Style: Throwing

Portuguese Knitting: Round the Neck

I'm a flicker, and I create my stitches by holding the working yarn over my right forefinger, and simply flicking the finger to wrap the yarn around the needle. To me it feels like the most efficient way of doing things, but that's only because it is what I have become used to. Many other knitters would disagree, arguing that their method is much more ergonomic.

English Style: Flicking [How I does it!]

None of this is really important, however, except that it's worth noting that the style I will be demonstrating in all the pictures in this book won't be any of those mentioned here, purely because I'm trying not to sway you one way or the other. I'll just be holding the yarn between thumb and forefinger, and manipulating it however I need to, without tensioning it around my fingers at all. You're under no pressure to develop *any* type of style just yet. That will come, and you'll probably find that you have evolved a variation of one of these styles all by yourself, without even realising how it happened. What matters is that whatever method you use, it needs to be one that feels the most comfortable to *you*.

As an aside, there are many other ways of knitting as well. Portuguese knitters carry their yarn around the neck or catch it on a particular type of pin attached to the lapel.

Many people find this a very fast and comfortable way to knit, particularly people who may have developed arthritis in their fingers: the finger movements in Portuguese knitting tend to be very small, and most of the work is done by the left thumb.

The list goes on and on, but let's not delay any further. Let's learn how to cast on!

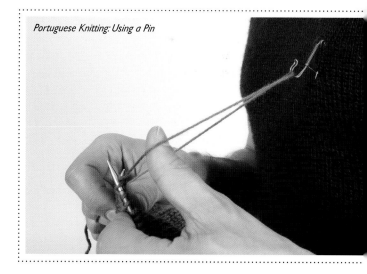

Portuguese Knitting: Using a Pin

SCAN T° WATCH
MY 'CAST °N' VID

STEP 1

Hold one of the knitting needles in your left hand, with the tip pointing towards your right, and place your new slip knot on the tip.

STEP 2

Pull on the tail end of the yarn, to tighten the knot around the needle. It doesn't want to be too tight, but you don't want it to be all loose and floppy, either.

STEP 3

Hold your knitting needles, one in each hand, rather like holding a knife and fork (but not the faux-posh way, where some people hold their knife like a pen…), with your hands over the top of the needles and the slip knot near the tip of the left needle. I hold the tail of the yarn in the fingers of my left hand to keep it out of the way.

TIP

One pitfall that many new knitters fall into is trying to keep everything *really* tight, so they don't lose control of it. This can lead to all sorts of problems, including painful tension in the jaw and shoulders, not to mention making it difficult to get your needle into the stitches! The aim is to maintain a nice even tension: not too tight that it becomes hard work and not too loose that your knitting has no structure.

At this early stage, I would say it is actually better to be too loose than too tight, as it's easier to tighten things up as you get better than it is to loosen up later on.

STEP 4

Insert the tip of the needle that is in your right hand (henceforward known as the 'right needle') into the loop nearest the tip of the left needle. (I know there's only one there now, but that's because this is the first time. When you repeat these steps, that instruction will make much more sense.) Make sure the right needle goes *underneath* the left needle, entering the loop from left to right. You want to finish with the two needle tips crossed. (Entering a stitch in this direction is called going in 'knitwise', or 'as if to knit'.)

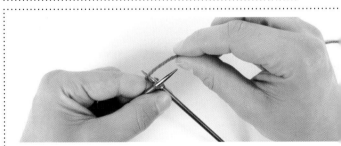

STEP 5

Pinch the two needles where they cross, with the left thumb and forefinger, to hold them steady. Using the now-free right hand, pick up the working yarn, and wrap it around the tip of the right needle, in an anticlockwise direction (as seen by looking down on the tip of the right needle). The yarn should now be coming towards you, between the two needle tips.

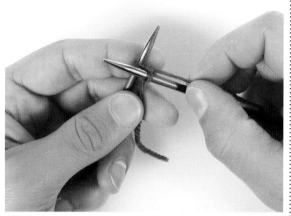

STEP 6

Keeping a nice steady tension on the working yarn, bring the tip of the right needle back towards you, and out of the loop it first went into, drawing with it a new loop of yarn created from the wrapping part of the previous step. You should now see that the right needle tip is lying on top of the left needle tip. (This one sounds tricky when explained in words, but it will make a lot more sense when you see it actually happening in front of you.)

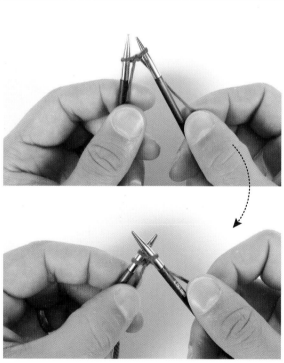

STEP 7

Now pivot the tip of the left needle, moving it in an anticlockwise direction, round to the front of the right needle, and insert it into the loop of yarn that is on the right needle, going into the loop from the right-hand side towards the left. (Think of the left needle tip making the longest journey it can before going into the loop on the right needle.)

STEP 8

Now slide the right needle out of the knitting completely, and you will see that you have created a new stitch on the left needle.

Congratulations! You have just completed your very first cast-on stitch! Repeat Steps 4–8, as many times as necessary, until you have the required amount of stitches on the left needle. Don't worry if all this feels a bit clumsy to begin with. You'll soon get the hang of it, and it will become second nature!

NB1: You can simply place the new stitch on the left needle the easiest way, without going all the way round to the front. The method described in Step 7, however, is the way I was always taught, and rather conveniently, it means you don't actually need to take the needle out at the end of creating a stitch at all (that's Step 8 obsolete, then!), just rotate the two needles around each other (in a way that will make much more sense when you try it for yourself), and adjust them so that they are in the same position as at the end of Step 4, ready to cast on another stitch. For that reason, I'll stick with my method, if you don't mind.

NB2: The original loop from the slip knot DOES count as your first stitch. For example, if you need ten stitches in total, you will only need to work these steps nine times.

THE KNIT STITCH

SCAN T° WATCH
MY 'KNIT STITCH' VID

The most basic unit of knitting is the knit stitch. You may also find people referring to it as a 'plain' stitch. If all you ever learn is how to create perfect knit stitches, you can still have a long and fulfilling relationship with knitting, and you'll still have the ability to make a variety of lovely things!

(But seriously, guys, why stop there? I only said that to let you know that this little stitch is a really important and useful thing to know, but let's get real: you are going to want a bit more flexibility than that!)

And do you want to know the best news of all? You've already pretty much learnt how to do it.

What?

You heard!

A knit stitch is not much different from the cast-on stitch that you have already become an expert at, with just one subtle change at the end. Even better: that change at the end is MUCH easier than the last two steps of the cast on!

Result!

The first three steps of creating the knit stitch are exactly the same as Steps 4–6 of the cast on in the previous section, but to recap, in simpler form (now that you are getting good at this), here they are again:

STEP 1
Insert the tip of the right needle into the first loop on the left needle, going in knitwise.

STEP 2
Wrap the working yarn anticlockwise around the tip of the right needle.

STEP 3
Bring the tip of the right needle towards you, coming out of the stitch and drawing with it a new loop of the wrapped yarn.

And *here's* where things are a little different. And a whole heap easier.

STEP 4
Slide the old stitch off the left needle, using the right needle tip to push it off the end.

Unlike how you ended the cast on, where you placed the new loop of yarn back onto the left needle, leaving the right needle free, this time you have the new loop of yarn—the new stitch—sitting on the right needle, and the two needles are both now still in the game.

To continue knitting, you simply repeat Steps 1–4, as described here, and each time you start a new stitch the right needle will go into whichever stitch is currently nearest to the tip of the left needle. Couldn't be simpler!

When you get to the last stitch in your row, you will knit into it, exactly like any other stitch you have encountered. As you complete the final stitch, and push the old stitch off the left needle, there will no longer be anything connecting the left needle to the right. You have completed your first row, and all of your stitches are now on the needle in your right hand. Does that sound like what you are looking at in your hands? I hope so. Otherwise you're odd, and we might not be able to be friends….

But I've now run out of stitches to knit, so what do I do next? Simply turn the knitting around, so that the needle tip is pointing towards the right, instead of towards the left, and hold it in your left hand. This is called 'turning the work'. You are now ready to start knitting again, going into what is now the first stitch on the left needle, exactly as you did at the start of the previous row.

As I said before, the knit stitch is such a fundamental component of knitting, and there is so much you could now do, with just the two skills you have already learnt. If you wanted to, you could ditch the rest of this book, and set about making yourself something like a simple scarf. You would just need to cast on enough stitches to make your scarf the width you want, and then, on every row, knit every single stitch. It's the simplest form of knitted scarf you could make, but it's one that has been in existence for centuries, and there's nothing wrong with that!

I suspect though, if you are anything like me, you are already thinking to yourself, 'Well, that was fun, and easier than I thought it would be. What can I learn next?'

(Truth be told, I feel obliged to say that if you *did* go off now to make a scarf like I've just mentioned, I reckon you'd end up being quite bored quite quickly. Don't get me wrong: there is something very soothing and meditative about the repetition of making knit stitch after knit stitch. I myself have made countless 'vanilla' socks, which are socks made entirely from knit stitches, with no other texture or technique at all, and I've always thoroughly enjoyed the process. They are usually just a palate cleanser though, for when I've got something more complicated 'on the needles'. Sometimes my brain is tired, but my fingers still want to knit. I rather suspect though, that you'll want a bit more variety in your knitting. After all, scarves are looooooooong…)

First row of knitting completed

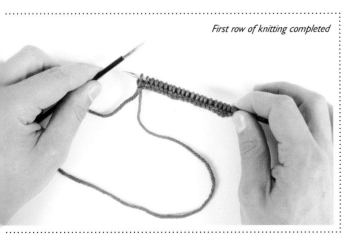

THE PURL STITCH

SCAN T° WATCH
MY 'PURL STITCH' VID

The next weapon in your knitter's arsenal—the brother tool in the crafty tool belt—is the purl stitch.

Now that you know how to handle your needles and your yarn, and you are getting pretty good with understanding what goes where, this should be a doddle.

You might be surprised to learn that a purl stitch is what a knit stitch looks like on the back. It therefore follows that a knit stitch is what a purl stitch looks like on the back. One is the reverse of the other.

Logically then, this means that much of what you do to create purls will be a sort of mirror image of what you did to create the knits in the last section.

GLºSSARY

Here's another vocab lesson (on top of the sneaky one I just slipped in, when I used **knits** and **purls** as shorter names for 'knit stitches' and, 'purl stitches'. Always in the game!): '**behind the work**' or '**at the back of the work**' (or sometimes, rather revoltingly, 'in back'—ugh!) means on the side of your knitting that is facing away from you, the knitter. '**In front of the work**' or '**at the front**' means on the side of the work facing you, the knitter. These terms are always taken from your own perspective, as you look at the work.

When you were making your knit stitches (or as it is actually called: *knitting*), you may have noticed that the working yarn was hanging down behind the work. This is correct. When you are knitting, the yarn hangs down at the back of the work. When you are *purling*, however, the yarn will be hanging down at the *front* of the work.

But why do I need to know this? Won't it just do what it needs to do anyway? Well, yes, it will, but if you aren't aware of the difference, you can get in a right tangle, particularly when you switch between knits and purls in the same row.

When you have been knitting and you need to switch to purling, you have to bring the yarn to the front of the work, i.e. towards you, before starting the first purl stitch. To do that, you simply bring it between the two needle tips, and let it hang out at the front.

The reverse is also true, so when you have been purling, and your next stitch is a knit stitch, you need to take the yarn away from you, again going back between the needle tips, to the back of the work, where it can hang out, ready for the first knit stitch.

If you don't do this, you will end up with errant strands of yarn looping over your needles, and if you aren't careful, chances are you'll knit into those loops on the next row and end up with more stitches in the row than you should have.

NB: Most people think that a beginner's most common error in knitting is dropping a stitch. It's actually the complete opposite, and people tend to accidentally gain more stitches than they want, through processes like I've just described. Fun fact, eh?

STEP 1

This is similar to Step 1 of the knit stitch, but we need to insert the right needle into the stitch in a totally different direction.

Insert the tip of the right needle into the next stitch on the left needle by coming towards you (from behind the work), and from the right-hand side of the loop. (Make sure that the right needle goes in *under* the left needle.)

STEP 2

This is pretty much the same as Step 2 of the knit stitch. The only difference here is that the right needle is in a different position.

Wrap the working yarn around the tip of the right needle in an anticlockwise direction.

STEP 3

Again, this is a sort of backwards version of what you do in Step 3 of the knit stitch. It's no more complicated, but it might seem a little tricky when described in words. If you remember how it felt to do this part of the knit stitch, that might help make this step seem a little more familiar.

Draw the tip of the right needle out of the stitch, going out the way you went in—which means the needle will be moving AWAY from you—taking the wrapped strand of yarn from Step 2 with it. The right needle will start this step in front of the left one, and end up behind it. There will be a new loop of yarn on the right needle.

STEP 4

Now, as with the knit stitch, using the side of the right needle, push the right needle towards your right, sliding the original loop off the tip of the left needle.

You are now in the enviable position of being able to do both a knit stitch AND a purl stitch! Suddenly a whole new world of possibility has opened up in front of you. There are many stitch patterns in knitting that are simply made up of combinations of just these two stitches. Stocking stitch, garter stitch, moss stitch, rib stitch: all of these are distinct textures that look and feel very different, but the one thing they all have in common? Knits and purls! You, my friend, are now well on your way!

The traditional fisherman's gansey is a type of thick, densely textured pullover worn at sea. It is usually patterned with intricate designs that are often made up only of knits and purls (although it's true some do feature cable stitches as well).

Take a look at the pic below: while the pattern on this gansey may look complex, it really is just knits and purls, both of which you know already. All right, admittedly, there's a little bit more involved in making a whole garment than just the few things you've learnt so far, but I'm talking specifically about the textures and patterns on the surface of the fabric itself. Knits and purls. That's all.

How amazing is that?!

CASTING °FF

(Also known as 'binding off', mostly in the US)

Once you've knitted as much as you want or need to, it's important to know what to do when you want to stop. It's like ice skating: it's all very well knowing how to go forward, and how to get up a good head of steam, but unless you know how to stop yourself you'll get into some serious bother…

If, for example, you simply took your newly completed piece of knitting off your needle, by sliding the needle out of the loops, you would soon find that all those loops of yarn you so painstakingly created would just unravel, and all that hard work would be lost in the blink of an eye.

Okay, so that's a little melodramatic. The stitches won't all miraculously undo themselves, but you will probably lose a few at the top of your work, and until you get more familiar with the structure of the fabric, understanding what goes where, you probably won't be able to rectify it. The end result will be the same: lost work, a fair few expletives colouring the air, and possibly, the urge to forget the whole thing entirely, and never pick up yarn and needles ever again. That's the *last* thing I want!

In order to finish your knitting safely, then, and ensure that none of those loops try to make a break for the border, we need to 'cast off' the work, successfully securing each loop across the top of the work so that nothing can go astray. As with most things in knitting, there are many ways to cast off—some are quite intricate, and like the different methods of casting on, can be very decorative—but for the purposes of what we will be learning in this book, I'm going to show you the very simplest version.

We don't necessarily need 'decorative' at this stage, but at some point, you might find it worth doing a little bit of searching around to see if you find a type of cast off that you prefer. And if you don't, that's fine too. This simple one will stand you in good stead for pretty much any situation you might find yourself in.

The concept is pretty simple: all the way along the top of your knitting, you will see that you have one loop of yarn for every stitch. They are all unfettered and free—it's only the knitting needle going through each one that holds them in place. We can change that state of affairs, by pulling each stitch through the one before it, effectively anchoring it in place. And as each subsequent stitch also gets anchored, the line of loops-pulled-through-loops gets ever more secure, until we reach the end of the row, when we will have dealt with all of them.

But how is it done? Hold onto your hat, we're going in…

STEP 1

As usual, at the start of a row, knit the first stitch. (I don't need to tell you how any more, do I?)

STEP 2

Nothing odd here either, simply knit the next stitch.

Now at this point, you will see that you have got two stitches on your right needle. Just checking you have, have you? Yes? Good. Now comes the actual casting off bit.

STEP 3

Insert the tip of the left needle into the front of the SECOND stitch on the right needle. That's the one furthest away from the needle tip, or to look at it another way, the rightmost one, or the first stitch that you knitted on this row. Insert the needle tip going into the stitch from the left to the right.

STEP 4

Now lift that second stitch over the first stitch on the right needle, and let it drop off the tip of the needle.

IMPORTANT: you must make sure that the other stitch remains on the needle as you do this. Be careful not to drop them both off at once.

In pulling the rightmost stitch over the leftmost, you have essentially done the same as if you had pulled the leftmost stitch *through* the rightmost. The end result is the same. Now you are back to having only one stitch on the right needle. The stitch that got dropped off the needle has now been successfully secured by the stitch that is coming through it, and won't be going anywhere untoward in a hurry.

That's it! That's genuinely all there is to it. To continue then, keep repeating Steps 2–4, until there are no stitches remaining on the left needle. You miss out Step 1 entirely each time, because after the first time through, you already have one stitch on the right needle.

STUFF T° KN°W

At this point, it's important to note that you need to make sure you don't work the cast off too tightly. You will have noticed that it is the nature of your knitted fabric to be very stretchy in all directions.

That's not the case with this cast off. If it isn't worked nice and loosely, it won't have enough give in it, and you will find that this end of your work will gather in quite a lot, and won't lie flat. This is particularly important if your cast off is at the neckline of a jumper, or the end of a sleeve, as you could easily find that you won't be able to fit your head or hand through the hole, and that would be a tragedy indeed!

With that in mind, then, just keep everything nice and loose as you work along your cast-off row: it's better to be too loose than too tight at this stage.

In a nutshell, the golden rule to remember is that every time you end up with two stitches on the right needle, you do the casting-off manoeuvre in Steps 3 and 4.

When the left needle is empty, and you have just completed your final Step 4, you will have one single stitch on the right needle. One final thing is now required to secure this last stitch, stopping it, and all the previous stitches, from unravelling back across the row.

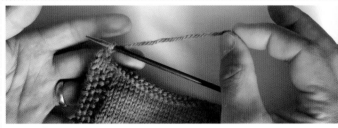

STEP 5

When you get to this point, cut the working yarn, leaving a 15cm (6in) tail for weaving in later.

STEP 6

Enlarge the loop that is on the right needle by gently pulling the needle away from the work, until the end pops free. Then pull on the tail, and this will tighten the loop. Everything is now locked in place. Your stitches are safe, and the knitting will not ever unravel.

NB: Just be sure not to pull everything *too* tight at this last point, as it's only that last loop that you want to close up. Otherwise you could distort a few of the stitches at the end of the row, and you don't want that.

You can now cast on, knit, purl, and cast off. That's not a bad haul for a beginner! Let's look at some of the different things you can do with these four basic-but-useful techniques in a little bit more detail.

W°RKING FLAT °R IN THE R°UND

So far, we've only focussed on the actual creation of individual stitches, and not put any emPHAsis on how those stitches relate to each other in any wider sense.

In your practice sample, you've just been knitting along a row. You'll remember that I've already given you instructions about how to 'turn the work' when you reach the end of a row and how to start the next row (page 47). Well, if you keep doing this, regardless of whether you are working with knit stitches or with purls, gradually your piece of knitting will grow and grow. It might become a square to put with lots of other squares to make a blanket or maybe it will get long enough to call a scarf. Whatever you do with it, you will see that you have been creating a flat piece of fabric. Without knowing it had a name, what you have been doing is called 'working flat', or 'knitting flat'. You may sometimes also hear this type of knitting referred to as 'working back and forth'.

So, what's knitting 'in the *round*'? It is, as you might expect, exactly what the name suggests. Rather than knitting back and forth, working on each side in turn, when working in the round, you cast on as many stitches as you require, in the normal fashion, but instead of turning the work and knitting the first row over the top of the stitches you have just cast on, you bring the two ends of your cast on around to meet each other. In doing so, you have formed a circle with your knitting, and you are ready to work in the round.

The major difference here is that you are going to be working round and round in a big spiral. There is no 'end of row'—just as a circle has no beginning and no end—it just keeps going. If you are a grammar pedant, such as I, I have no doubt that you would rather refer to the method as 'knitting in a spiral' instead of 'knitting in the round'. I know *I* would.

GL°SSARY

There are many terms in knitting that strike me as inaccurate, cumbersome, or not particularly user-friendly. I constantly bicker (lovingly) with my technical editor, and say things like, 'But why SHOULDN'T it be written my way? It makes so much more SENSE!'

She very patiently sighs, and says, 'Yes, I know, but things just aren't done like that, and you are dealing with people who have been reading knitting patterns for twice as long as you've been alive.'

She has a point. And I always defer to her better judgement.

I mention knitting in a spiral only *partly* facetiously. One of the things that needs to be explained when teaching people about knitting in the round is this very fact. You are not actually making rings of knitting, but one continuous spiral all the way up the tube of your knitting.

This has a knock-on effect on things like stripes. Because of the nature of a spiral, completed 'rounds*' of knitting don't finish in line with where they start. The *end* of a round instead sits one layer of stitches higher than the *beginning* of the same round.

This can (read: does!) cause a visible 'jog' in the work, perhaps where your yarn has changed colour, or maybe where a textured pattern of stitches wraps from one round to the next. It's not a flaw, just a feature of the technique.

When I first learnt how to knit, I was obsessed with trying to minimise this jog as much as I could. There are ways to reduce its effect, but to be honest, I now just embrace the fact that the jogs exist, and as a result, my life is a lot less stressful!

*When not working flat, we don't talk about 'rows', instead we say, 'rounds'.

But hang on, you reasonably protest; my knitting needles are straight, and they do not bend. How can I possibly bring one end of the cast on round to meet the other, without snapping the darned things? You raise a very good point.

DPNs are an ingenious way of getting around this stumbling block. (You've already learnt they come in sets, and usually in sets of five.) Wherever two needles meet, they form a 'hinge' of sorts. Dividing your total number of stitches between *four* needles gives you *three* hinges, thus enabling you to bring the two ends of your cast on around to meet each other. Admittedly, it's more of a square than a circle (call it a 'squircle', if you must), but you get the point. The fourth hinge is created where the start of the cast on meets the end.

Now that your stitches are in the form of a closed ring, albeit a square one (sheesh, stop whining: I get it!), you can knit your way along the first side of the squircle, using the fifth needle as your working needle. When you get to the end of that first needle, to the first hinge, all the stitches from that first side will be on the working needle, and the one that originally held them will have come free. As you work along the *second* side of the square, the now-free needle takes a turn as the working needle.

Keep repeating this pattern all the way around the square, until you get to the end of the fourth side. Then start work on the next round with the current free needle (I KNOW! It's a square!), and you're on your way again.

With this method, you never turn the work, so you won't ever be working on the opposite side of the fabric.

To clarify, when knitting in the round, you always work on the *outside* of the tube, never the inside.

Want to have a go? Good. I'll take you through it, step by step, in just a tick.

It's perfectly possible to cast on your stitches onto each needle in turn, but to be honest, it's a lot easier to cast on the total number of stitches onto one, single DPN, then you can slip them from that needle onto the others, until they are evenly distributed.

Ah. Slipping stitches: that's something we haven't talked about yet. Probably best to do that before we go any further.

SLIPPING STITCHES

Slipping a stitch means simply transferring it from one needle to the other, without working it in any way. You don't knit it and you don't purl it: you just slip it over from one tip to the other.

I'd love to say it was as simple as that, but there are four different ways that you can slip a stitch*, depending on what outcome you want to have. You can go from the left needle to the right, or from the right needle to the left. A stitch can also be slipped either knitwise or purlwise. Let's look at the steps for all of those options.

SCAN T° WATCH
MY 'SLIPPING STITCHES' VID

STEP 2
Now slide the stitch off the end of the left needle, transferring it to the right one.

SLIPPING FR°M LEFT NEEDLE T° RIGHT, KNITWISE

STEP 1
Insert the tip of the right needle into the next stitch on the left needle, going in from left to right, and from front to back. *Psst!: It's the same as starting a knit stitch…*

SLIPPING FR°M LEFT NEEDLE T° RIGHT, PURLWISE

STEP 1
Insert the tip of the right needle into the next stitch on the left needle, coming in from back to front, and from right to left, as if you were about to perform a purl stitch.

STEP 2
Now slide the stitch off the end of the left needle, transferring it to the right one.

Of course, you might at some point need to slip the stitches in the opposite direction, i.e. from the right needle to the left.

That's not as unusual as you might think. In fact, I specify this very manoeuvre in many of my patterns, so it's definitely worth knowing.

STUFF T° KN°W
Slipping a stitch knitwise (or, 'as if to knit') in either direction, *remounts* the stitch, meaning it sits differently on the needle. This is something you may or may not wish to do. We'll chat more about the anatomy of a stitch in Chapter 7 (see page 80), but it's useful to be aware it's a thing!

For the sake of detail, you may or may not care to know that slipping a stitch knitwise from left needle to *right* rotates it *anticlockwise*, whereas slipping it knitwise from *right* needle to left rotates it *clockwise*. Now you know. (Whether you cared to or not.)

SLIPPING FR°M RIGHT NEEDLE T° LEFT, KNITWISE

(Remember: slipping knitwise remounts the stitch)

STEP 1

This is a little different from what you have done before, but it's no more complicated. Insert the tip of the left needle into the first stitch on the right needle, going in from right to left, and from front to back.

STEP 2

Slide the stitch off the tip of the right needle, transferring it to the left needle.

You can probably work out the mechanics of the fourth method all by yourself now, but just so that you don't have to…

SLIPPING FR°M RIGHT NEEDLE T° LEFT, PURLWISE

STEP 1

Insert the tip of the left needle into the first stitch on the right needle, going in from left to right, and from back to front.

STEP 2

Slide the stitch off the tip of the right needle, transferring it to the left needle.

Right, sorry about that little detour, but definitely worth the read!

Let's get back to what we were *supposed* to be talking about, which is how to cast on in the round using DPNs!

Remember that?

If I'm being completely honest, there are actually twelve different ways to slip a stitch. The four described above can be done with the yarn either at the back of the work or at the front, for different results, and don't get me started about slipping as if to purl through the back loop! I think that's going a bit too far in these early days, don't you?

CASTING ⁰N IN THE R⁰UND USING DPNS

SCAN T⁰ WATCH MY 'CASTING ⁰N IN THE R⁰UND USING DPNS' VID

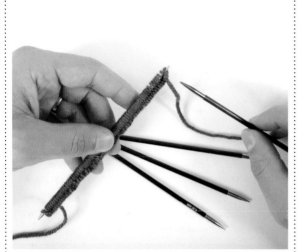

STEP 1

Let's assume you want to cast on 80 stitches: it's a nice, useful number to work with! Starting with a slip knot, cast on 79 stitches onto a single DPN, using a second one as your working needle. (79 stitches plus the slip knot, makes 80 stitches in total, natch…)

When you have cast on all your stitches, you should have the needle holding them all in your left hand. The working yarn should be hanging from the right-hand end, while the tail (where you started the cast on) should be hanging from the left-hand end.

STEP 2

Slip 20 stitches from the left needle to the right, purlwise.

STEP 3

Keep hold of the needle that is in your left hand and let go of the one in your right. Don't worry about it running off anywhere: the physics of friction means that those 20 sts will hold it in place perfectly well.

Pick up a third needle in your right hand.

STEP 4

Slip the next 20 stitches from the left needle over to that third needle, purlwise. You can ignore the hanging needle completely. It still won't be going anywhere, honest.

STEP 5

Let go of the needle that is in your right hand, and pick up a fourth DPN, and with it, slip a *further* 20 stitches from the left needle onto it. It's purlwise again, because we don't want to remount the stitches.

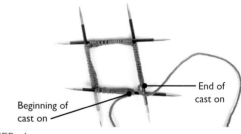

End of cast on

Beginning of cast on

STEP 6

You now have 20 sts on each of four needles. Being careful not to let the cast-on stitches twist around the needles in any way, arrange the four needles into a square, so that the beginning of the cast on comes around to meet the end.

Describing this next bit makes it sound a whole lot trickier than it really is, so bear with me…

Locate the point where you began your cast on (see the short yarn tail? It's there). That's the needle that should be in your left hand, and the tail should be dangling from the right-hand end. The needle in your right hand (for now) should be the one with the working yarn hanging from it. Additionally, the working yarn should be coming from the left-hand end of the needle.

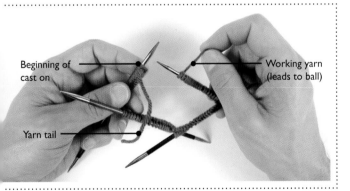

Beginning of cast on

Working yarn (leads to ball)

Yarn tail

When holding these two needles in your knitting position, the point where they cross is the point where the two ends of your cast on come together, transforming a horseshoe into the perfect squircle, at last.

Don't worry about the other two needles for now. They'll carry on doing what they are doing until a bit later. It's best to ignore them completely. Then you only have to deal with two needles at a time, just like the process you're already used to. Don't get me wrong, those extra needles, the little blighters, will do

their absolute best to get in your way. Just like coping with a naughty nephew, however, not giving them the satisfaction of any attention at all is by far the best way to encourage good behaviour!

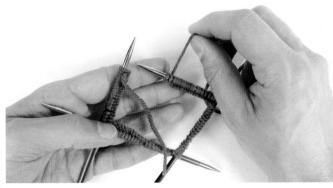

STEP 7

As you look down at the two needles that you are holding, it's important that the working yarn is hanging down at the back of the work for making the next knit stitch. (It's certainly not unheard of to start a round with a purl stitch. In that case, you need to bring the working yarn to the front. That's not the situation here, but it happens once or twice in a couple of the patterns in this very book!)

When working in the round, the 'back of the work' actually means the surface on the *inside* of your knitted tube. That said, the yarn shouldn't be coming up *through the centre* of your four needles. We just want it coming from over the top of the stitches that are on the needle in your right hand, and from behind the work as a whole.

STEP 8

With your left thumb and forefinger, pinch the two needles where they cross, just to hold everything steady. Now you can let go with your right hand, without risking everything falling apart.

Pick up the fifth needle. It will be your working needle for the next stage.

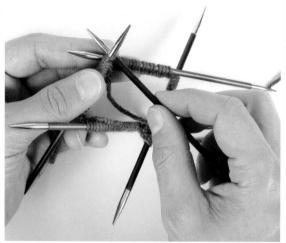

STEP 9

Insert the working needle into the first stitch on the left needle, ready to make the first knit stitch.

STEP 10

Wrap the yarn, draw through, and slip off, to complete the stitch. Creating this first stitch successfully connects one end of the cast on to the other.

Keep repeating Steps 9 and 10, until you have worked all the stitches on that first needle. What *was* the working needle has now been incorporated into the round with the others, and the needle you were working *from* is now free to become the working needle for the next side.

Continuing around the square in the same direction, adjust the needles in your hands so that the working yarn is once again hanging off the left-hand end of the needle that is now to the right of the one currently in your left hand. Insert the new working needle into the first stitch on the new left needle, and off you go again. Keep going in this manner to the end of the round.

NB: You will no doubt find that there is quite a gap at the start of the round, where the stitches at the start and at the end have pulled away from each other. This is perfectly normal, and after you have worked a couple more rounds, it will probably close up on its own. The more you get used to this, the more you'll get a handle on it, but the main thing here is not to try to work around that corner REALLY TIGHTLY. Although that might feel logical, it will actually make matters worse. Let your knitting find its own tension here, as everywhere else, and all will be well.

It's time for a bit of a confession here: I *never* use DPNs for working in the round.

What? Then why have you gone to all that trouble, teaching me how to knit that way, if there's no point to it?

There absolutely IS a point. I keep saying that there are many ways of doing things in knitting and working in the round is no exception. There are many knitters who swear by using DPNs and wouldn't be happy doing anything else. I think it's right that I should give you as many options as possible. That way, you can make up your own mind about what method suits you best.

I have to say, there is also a little part of me that likes feeling connected to the traditional ways of doing things. It's almost like you can feel a tangible line going back through the centuries, joining you to those knitting pioneers who first discovered the wonderful things that you can do with two sticks and a length of yarn. The romantic in me loves all that shit, even though the scientist in me keeps telling me to get over myself and look at how far things have moved on.

Science aside for a sec though, although we might have needles made of different materials these days. The fact remains that the mechanics of using a set of DPNs for working in the round haven't changed a jot in some seven hundred years, so it must be pretty good, no?

If I don't use DPNs then, what *do* I do when working in the round?

MAGIC LP

Magic, uh… what now? It's a bit of a stupid name, admittedly, but magic loop is just a different method of working in the round. It does exactly the same job, but instead of using four or five DPNs, you use a single, circular needle.

(You know, the ones with two short metal tips connected by a flexible cable or cord? Remember? Thank goodness for that…)

You need a needle with a pretty long cable for working magic loop.

If you think about it, the circular needle is a bit like your set of DPNs, once you have got some in-the-round knitting on them, except that instead of having the DPNs meet each other in the corners all around the work, here, you have one continuous cable running all the way round the circle.

STEP 1

Casting on for magic loop is not really any different from casting on for DPNs. You still cast on the number of stitches required for the round, all in a line. It's just that this time, you are using the two tips of a circ, rather than two DPNs. Go on then: cast on 80 sts onto your circ!

STEP 2

Next, slide all of the stitches (being careful not to let them twist) onto the flexible cable.

STEP 3

The likelihood is that you'll want to divide the stitches into two groups (roughly or equally: that depends on how anal you are, and on your relationship with your own conscience…).

Find the spot where you want to divide your stitches, slightly pull two of them apart, take hold of the cable nestling between them, and pull it, so that a loop of the cable sticks out between them. This is the loop of the magic loop. Clever, huh? So, where's the magic? That's a bit trickier. (See my earlier comment about it being a bit of a stupid name.)

NB: You might find it's easier to get the loop of cable out if you fold the line of stitches in half, cast-on edge to cast-on edge.

This is the line along the bottom of your work, opposite the edge that is made from the loops on the cable.

The stitches will part quite naturally at the midway point (ish). Just be careful not to put an actual fold into the cable itself: you'll damage it, and your cable will end up annoyingly kinky.

(Far be it from me, of course, to describe anyone's kinks as annoying, but if you are a kinky knitting-needle cable, you're annoying!)

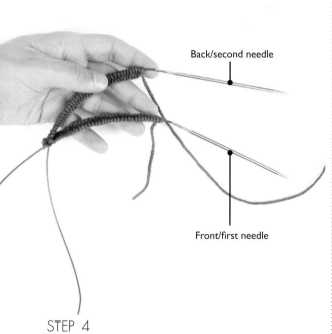

Back/second needle

Front/first needle

STEP 4

With the two cast-on edges facing in towards each other, hold your needles so that the tips are pointing to the right, and the loop is towards the left. One of the needles will naturally sit above the other, or depending on how you hold them, further away from you.

The top (or further) needle is called the back needle, and the other needle, the lower (or nearer) one, is called the front needle.

(Sometimes the front needle is called the first needle, and the back needle is called the second needle. Whatever words are used, it's bound to be something that is obviously descriptive.)

It's important that the working yarn is hanging from the back needle at this point. If it isn't, juggle things around until it is.

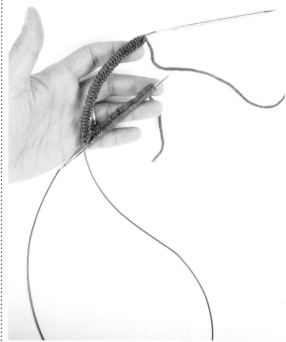

STEP 5

Being careful not to let anything twist, slide the stitches that are currently on the front half of the cable onto the front needle tip.

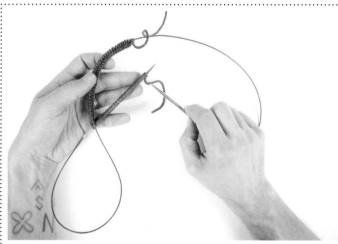

STEP 6

Pull the back needle long, until there is enough cable free for you to bring the tip around to your normal knitting position.

NB: At this point, you need to make sure that the working yarn is in the correct position for your first stitch. Assuming that you are about to do a knit stitch, rather than a purl, the working yarn needs to be hanging down at the back of the work. If it's already there, bingo! If, however, it is hanging down at the *front* of the work, or rather, in between the two halves of the cast on, then you need to take it over the back section of the cable, to the back to the work, ready to knit with.

Now you are all set up and ready to go!

STEP 7

Insert the tip of what has now become the right needle (it was the back needle!) into the first stitch on what is now the left needle (it was the front needle!) and knit it as normal.

NB: Just as with working on DPNs, it's easy for a big gap to appear at the start of the round. Again, this will no doubt sort itself out after a couple of rounds have been worked, but it's a good idea to pay attention to keeping your tension nice and even so that things don't get too loose.

Continue knitting all the stitches along that first side of the work (more commonly described as something like 'work all the stitches on the current—or first—needle').

STEP 8

When you get to the end of the first needle, the left needle will come free from the work.

The right needle, containing the stitches, will be pointing to the left.

Turn the work so that it once again points to the right.

*This pic is a bit like Michelangelo's 'The Creation of Adam', don't you think? Anyone? No? Just me, then...

STEP 9

Half of your stitches will be on one of the needle tips and the other half will be on the cable. Make sure that the ones that are on the needle tip are further away from you, and the ones on the cable are nearer to you.

STEP 10*

Once again, make sure that the working yarn (it will be on the back needle) is behind the work (i.e. lying over the *top* of the back needle). Then slide the stitches from the cable onto the front needle tip.

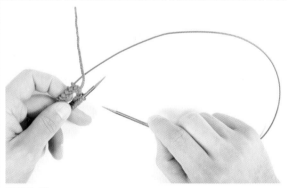

STEP 11

Pull the back needle long, until you again have enough spare cable to be able to hold the needle in position to knit with once more. Carry on knitting to the end of the round. (Starting a new round is no different from turning the work halfway through.)

A PERSONAL MESSAGE

This is not said in any way to try to influence a new knitter (that's you!). It's just so you know where I'm coming from. I'm a total, 100%-dyed-in-the-wool magic looper! As I said before, I never use DPNs for knitting in the round, and even though I own several sets, I often wonder why I bought them, as I could get by perfectly well without ever touching one. I don't mean to contradict what I said earlier about liking the nostalgia and tradition that goes hand in glove with using them either. It's all true, but for many reasons, I much prefer magic loop, and all my socks, hats, and anything else that needs to be worked in the round (even jumpers!) are always done that way. Forget the silly name, it's the method that works best for me.

For balance's sake, of course, both methods have their pluses and minuses. DPNers would argue that all that pushing and pulling of the needle tips at the halfway and end points of the round slows things down too much. Loopers will counter that it only happens twice per round, whereas you reach a 'corner' with DPNs *four* times per round. Loopers will crow that you can't drop one of your tips down the side of the sofa, because they are joined together, while DPNers…um…have no answer to that! And for me, that's enough! Sold!

Seriously though, some knitters will swear that magic loop is more prone to causing little ladders in the corners, because the angle at which the two halves of the knitting fold onto each other is more acute than when using DPNs. I don't subscribe to that as a valid argument at all. It's perfectly possible, with care, to have no visible ladders whatsoever using either technique. I suspect a lot of what people say is based on their own experience, which in turn is based on possible individual circumstances (dare I say: flaws? Issues?) in their own knitting, which can lead to certain less-than-desirable outcomes.

That's actually good advice for pretty much everything in the knitting world. There are as many different opinions on things as there are knitters floating about, and the best advice I can give you is to go and find as many different answers to your questions as you possibly can. Try them all out and see which one gives you the most successful outcome.

Oh, that, of course, and listen to me, because everything I say is obviously correct…

For me, one big advantage to using magic loop is its portability. I often knit on the Tube or on the bus, while getting around London, and it's so easy—even mid-round—to hurriedly pull the tips out of your knitting, letting the stitches rest safely on the cable. Then you can stuff the whole caboodle into a bag, or even your pocket! You can be 100% confident that your stitches won't find their way off the needles. They will be happily waiting there for you when you have completed your transfer between the Northern and Victoria Lines at Euston Station!

That leads me onto another huge plus: the cable is usually a lot thinner than the tips that you are using. If you leave your knitting alone for a few days (I'm laughing as I type that, because when you *really* get into this, that's the LAST thing you'll want to do), leaving the stitches on the needle tips will actually stretch the yarn a little bit. Maybe not much, but once you knit past that point, don't be surprised to find a little visible ridge across your work, where the stretched stitches are a little bit bigger than the others. It can be hugely frustrating, when all this time, you have been so mindful of maintaining even tension in your work.

Sliding your stitches onto the thinner cable between knitting sessions eliminates this problem entirely. The much thinner cable allows the yarn in those resting stitches to relax, rather than to be held under stress. It's these little details that can make the difference between a piece that you are proud of and one that bugs you every time you see it.

Also, you won't ever get your knitting out, ready to enjoy working a few rounds on your lunch break, only to find that you have lost a DPN, and can't continue until you can replace it.

ARGH!

Okay, so I sound a little biased. That's only because, in the matters that are important to me, magic loop comes up with the goods. *Your* priorities, however, may be different from mine, so don't rule out DPNs just because I prefer another way!

USING TWO CIRCULAR NEEDLES

Another way of working in the round is to use two circular needles concurrently, rather than just one, as in magic loop.

In the interests of page space, I've decided not to discuss it, as it's not as popular, or as commonplace a method as the two described above. It's definitely worth knowing that it exists, though, and if you want to do some homework to find out more, just Google 'knitting in the round with two circular needles', and you can make up your own mind as to whether you think it is something you want to try or not.

SIMPLE STITCH TEXTURES

With the skills you have already learnt, there are already many different stitch textures that you can utilise to create interesting and beautiful designs in your knitting. Some of them are deceptive: they might look very complex, but you'll be amazed at the level of detail that can be achieved using only knits and purls. Some, on the other hand, are very simple indeed, and those are the ones that we shall be looking at in this section.

HAZARD
One of the peculiar quirks of knitting is that many of the different textures you can create need to be made one way if knitted flat, and a totally different way if worked in the round.

A big part of why this makes a difference is the fact that you are either working on *both* sides of the fabric or on just one. We've already ascertained that a stitch that presents itself as a knit stitch on one side of the fabric looks like a purl on the other, and vice versa.

That's why it matters whether you are working on one side or two.

STOCKING STITCH

Easily the simplest of all stitch patterns, certainly in terms of its appearance, stocking stitch is probably the most familiar knitted texture out there. Whenever anyone imagines a knitted fabric, it's most likely to be this stitch that they are picturing.

When you look at the 'right side' of a piece of fabric made in stocking stitch, you will see that it looks like a whole heap of little 'Vs'. Every stitch looks like the letter V, and they are all arranged in perfect rows and columns, stacking up on top of each other nicely and standing shoulder to shoulder with the stitches on either side.

Turn it over to look at the 'wrong side' of the fabric, and you'll see it looks very different. Here, the fabric is entirely covered with little horizontal bumps of yarn. You might notice that they look a lot like the stitches that you made when you were purling. In fact, that's exactly what they are, and we even call them 'purl bumps'. (That should give you some clue as to how stocking stitch is created!)

GLOSSARY
When we talk about the **'right side'** or **'wrong side'** of your knitting, we are alluding to the fact that one side of the work often looks better than the other. Patterns are usually designed to make sure that all the attractive stuff happens on the side that people will see, called the 'right' side, and all the stuff that you might want to hide away out of sight will be on the 'wrong' side.

Most often, you will begin your knitting on the right side. This is not by any means, however, a hard and fast rule.

NB: It's also worth noting that certain patterns are deliberately reversible, and terms like 'right side' and 'wrong side' therefore don't really apply. My very own Ski Lift Scarf pattern (page 150) is a good example of that.

What you are seeing is this: the right side of stocking stitch is made from knit stitches, and the wrong side is made from purl stitches.

Consequently, when you are working flat, the first row (the right-side row, abbreviated to 'RS') will be all knit.

When you turn the work, you then need to *purl* that second row (the wrong side, or 'WS'). That's what makes the stitches on the right side show as knit stitches. With me? That's just logic.

So, the pattern for working stocking stitch flat is this:

Row 1 (RS):   Knit all stitches.
Row 2 (WS):   Purl all stitches.

Repeat Rows 1 and 2, alternating.

When working in the round, however, there *is* no turning of the work, meaning you'll never be working on a wrong side. Consequently, you don't need to work any purl stitches at all, and as a result, the pattern is even simpler.

Round 1:   Knit all stitches.

Repeat Round 1.

Nice.

I have always assumed (without any facts to back up this assumption) that the name 'stocking stitch' comes from the fact that stockings are traditionally worked in the round, and the simplest thing to do in the round is just keep knitting.

In the US, stocking stitch is called stockinette, and that can lead to some confusion. Anecdotally, I have been led to believe that there was originally a distinction between the two, and that the stitch itself was called stocking stitch while the *fabric created by stocking stitch* was called stockinette. This distinction seems to have fallen out of use, which is a shame, as it clears up a lot of ambiguity as far as I can see.

HAZARD

Stocking stitch has a real tendency to curl up on itself, both horizontally and vertically. This can be *incredibly* annoying, particularly in light of the fact that the texture of stocking stitch is my absolute favourite, and so pleasing to the eye, due to its uniformity and neatness.

The curling happens because of the marked difference between the two sides. One side wants to take up much more space than the other and pushes its counterpart round the corners! I say 'one side' because looking at it logically, the side with the purl bumps looks like it *should* be the one that does the pushing. In fact, it's both. The right side curls back on itself at the sides, suggesting that it must be the width of the knit stitches that is causing the curl, while the wrong side curls forwards, at the top and the bottom. I can't find a single reason why that should be the case, but I have to accept that it is! I suspect it will take one of the physicists among you out there to figure out why. If you come up with an answer, do let me know!

GARTER STITCH

Garter stitch looks *very* different from stocking stitch. For starters, the two sides of the fabric look identical. You can see (above) that the texture is made from horizontal ridges of purl bumps, with narrow furrows in between them. You might also notice that the same number of rows of garter stitch won't be as tall as their stocking-stitch counterparts. That's quite correct, as garter stitch definitely compresses itself vertically in a way that stocking stitch does not.

Looked at in more detail, those furrows between the ridges are actually rows of knit stitches, nestling in between the rows of purls. If you pull these rows apart vertically you'll see all those little knit stitches hiding away in there. Let go of the fabric and the furrows spring shut once more. Bouncy, isn't it?

I think one of the best features of garter stitch is that bounce, or spring. It tends to be a much thicker, squishier fabric than stocking stitch can produce, and as a result, it's great for shawls and scarves, where you want to trap as much air as possible inside the fabric for insulation purposes.

So how is it made? It's actually no more complicated than stocking stitch. Worked flat, it couldn't be simpler. Looking at

the right side—not a very appropriate term in this instance, as garter stitch creates a reversible fabric—you want to alternate between a row of knit stitches and a row of purl stitches. Start with the row of knits. Then turn the work, and for the second row to show up on the *other* side as *purl* stitches, they need to be created on *this* side as knits.

What? RS and WS rows are both knitted?

Yep! That's right! Your pattern for garter stitch worked flat, therefore, is:

- Row 1 (RS): Knit all stitches.
- Row 2 (WS): Knit all stitches.

- Repeat Rows 1 and 2, alternating.

Even *that* makes it look more complicated than it actually is: regardless of which row you are on, just knit every stitch.

Now for garter stitch worked in the round. Again, we want to build up alternating rows of knits and purls, but here, crucially, we won't be turning the work. Logic dictates, therefore, that we need to work one complete round of knit stitches followed by one round of purls, and the pattern for that looks like this:

- Round 1: Knit all stitches.
- Round 2: Purl all stitches.

- Repeat Rounds 1 and 2, alternating.

One great thing about garter stitch? It doesn't curl at all. It lies completely flat, and that is due to it being the same on both sides. Each side contains equal numbers of knits and purls, resulting in the VERY useful property of flatness!

If a pattern calls for large portions of stocking stitch, you'll often add a border of garter stitch to combat curling. Even if the border is just three stitches wide, or six rows tall, it still does the job very nicely.

M°SS STITCH

Moss stitch is also something you can already do, you just don't know it yet.

Everything that you have done so far has included an entire row of one particular stitch, or an entire row of another. This is where we start to mix things up a touch and ramp up the jeopardy! (I kid, of course: there ain't a great deal of jeopardy in knitting: nothing happens very quickly and even though any mistakes can be fixed or undone, my publisher wanted to inject a bit of a thrill at this point…)

Like garter stitch, moss stitch creates a completely curl-free fabric, making it, too, very useful for edging sections of stocking stitch. It looks and feels very different from garter stitch, which is all about horizontal ridges.

Moss stitch is all criss-crossy.

Each row is made from alternating one knit stitch and one purl stitch. On the next row, you knit into each purl stitch and purl into each knit stitch. Consequently, the knits and purls are offset from each other by one stitch, and that's what creates all those diagonal lines of purl bumps.

This means, of course, that you will have to switch between knitting and purling in the same row. Shock horror! I told you, man: jeopardy! It's actually not hard at all, as long as you remember that the working yarn needs to be at the back of the work for each knit stitch, and at the front for each purl. It means you'll be moving the yarn forwards or backwards after every stitch.

The pattern repeat is just two stitches, one knit, and one purl: [K1, P1]. Here it is, written as you might come across it in a pattern:

Row 1 (RS): *K1, P1; repeat from * to end of row.
Row 2 (WS): *P1, K1; repeat from * to end of row.

Repeat Rows 1 and 2, alternating.

Hang on: if the first row ends with a purl, and the second row *starts* with a purl, won't the purls and knits stack on top of each other, and we'll end up with columns? It's a good question, and seems perfectly logical, but it's not correct. Remember that when knitted flat, a stitch created as a knit stitch on one side, now presents itself on the other as a purl stitch. The reverse is also true: what was created on one side as a purl stitch now presents itself on the other as a knit stitch.

That being the case, the last stitch of the first row—a purl—is now showing up as a knit stitch, after turning the work. *That's* why you purl the first stitch of the second row, because it is being worked into a stitch that looks like a knit. Even though it was made as a purl.

If that's all just too confusing, you can look at things in simpler terms, and just say that after laying down the first row of alternating knits and purls, on all subsequent rows, just knit the purls, and purl the knits. Easy peasy. (And if even *that's* too much, just follow the instructions, and try not to think about it too hard.)

As with garter stitch, you work it differently depending on whether you are knitting flat or in the round. It goes further than that, though, because it also matters whether you are working with an odd or an even number of stitches.

Don't worry too much about that: just remember to keep alternating, working the knits into the purls and the purls into the knits. That way, you won't go far wrong.

I should probably, rather grudgingly, tell you that moss stitch is sometimes called 'seed stitch'. It's certainly the prevailing term in the US. As far as I can work out, there is no difference in how the stitch is worked, it just has a different name. Helpful.

In the knitting world, you'll often find that two different things have the same name, or that one thing has two different names. Having no standard language and so many regional discrepancies can make reading a pattern a bit of a minefield. Hopefully, all the information you need will be included in the pattern, but if in doubt, try to look at pictures of the finished object to see which version of a particular contentious term the designer intended.

RIBBING

Okay, my intrepid and gung-ho knitting brethren: now we're getting down to business! And this subject is such a doozy, it almost warrants a chapter all of its own.

Ribbing, like moss stitch, is a combination stitch, but this one shows up as neat columns of knit and purl stitches working across the row.

There are many different types of rib: even or uneven combinations of knits and purls create lots of different effects, but they all come under the same umbrella.

2x2 RIB

To begin with, I want to talk about what I refer to as '2x2 rib' (which you would say out loud as 'two by two rib').

You might also see it called 'K2P2 rib', or some other name that is basically just a descriptive term for whatever type of rib you are talking about.

2x2 rib shows in the work as a two-stitch-wide column of knits, followed by a two-stitch-wide column of purls, hence, '2x2'.

When working 2x2 rib, it's best to cast on a multiple of four stitches, i.e. 20, 24, 28, 32, 36, etc. This is the first time that we'll be dealing with a 'repeated stitch pattern' (or 'pattern repeat', or simply, a 'repeat'—call it what you will), and keeping the numbers simple makes life a whole lot more fun.

Here's how it's done, worked flat:

STEP 1

With the working yarn at the back of the work, knit two stitches.

STEP 2

Bring the working yarn to the front of the work, between the two needle tips. It is now ready to work the next stitch, which will be a purl stitch.

STEP 3

Purl two stitches.

STEP 4

Now you can return the working yarn to the back of the work, again going between the two needles. This takes it to the correct position for working the next (knit) stitch.

Repeat Steps 1–4 across the row.

You will have finished the last row with two purl stitches. Turn the work, and those two purl stitches now present themselves to you as knit stitches. Starting the row with two knit stitches, then, means that the knits stack up on top of the knits, and the purls—you guessed it—stack up on top of the purls. Stacking up the alternating knits and purls in this manner is what creates those distinctive columns.

We're okay with 2x2 ribbing, then, but what about other types? There are loads—way too many to go into here—but let's have a look at some of the more common ones.

1x1 RIB

As I'm sure you can probably guess, this is a type of rib that is worked with one knit stitch followed by one purl stitch. There's actually no reason why it shouldn't be one purl stitch followed by one knit stitch, but it's much more common to see ribbing instructions written with the knit stitches first. That said, I have been known to split things up a bit, for reasons of symmetry, instructing people to perhaps:

: *P1, K2, P1; repeat from * to end of row.

That's just another way of getting 2x2 rib—the last P of the repeat, and the following first P of the repeat sit next to each other, creating the same effect as 'P2'—so don't be surprised if what appears to be the most logical way of writing the repeat isn't always what you see in front of you in a pattern. You'll see this exact scenario in two of the patterns at the back of this book, and I've done it to make sure that all the stitches line up the way I want them to.

2x1 RIB

Logically, this is 'K2, P1'. Exactly as you'd expect.

1x2 RIB

You'd think this might just be a different way of writing 2x1 rib. Actually, it's not. This one is asking you to 'K1, P2', meaning that there is only one knit stitch (rather than two), alternating with two purl stitches (rather than just one).

NB: Although the RS of this stitch pattern looks exactly the same as the WS of 2x1 rib (strengthening the argument that they are in fact the same stitch pattern), there are plenty of occasions when this particular effect might be needed on the RS of a pattern, so that's why it exists as a rib combination in its own right.

3x1, 3x2, 4x2, ETC.

Basically, any combination of two whole numbers can be rendered as a type of rib stitch. You are only limited here by your imagination. And by the scope of the current understanding of number theory.

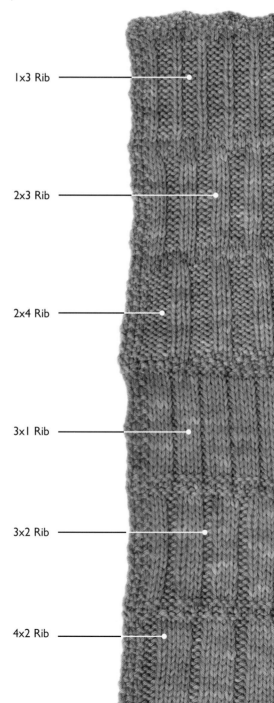

1x3 Rib

2x3 Rib

2x4 Rib

3x1 Rib

3x2 Rib

4x2 Rib

WORKING WITH PATTERN REPEATS AND SPECIFIC NUMBERS OF STITCHES

A repeated stitch pattern could include any number of stitches. 2x2 rib happens to be a four-stitch repeat, but you might be working a repeat that contains a 104 stitches. To make sure the stitches of your repeats all stack on top of each other the way they are supposed to, you need to have the correct number of stitches in your row.

But what if you have, say, 30 stitches on your needle, and you want to work a four-stitch repeat? Your four-stitch repeat covers 28 of the 30 stitches on your needle, but that still leaves two stitches to find a home for. You could decide to split them up, with one extra stitch at each end row, or you could choose to keep them together, and send them to the end of the row, essentially creating an extra half repeat *after* the main repeated section.

Either option will do the trick, but bear in mind that if you choose the latter, once you have turned the work, you must remember that those two extra stitches will be at the START of the following row, and will need to be dealt with *before* you begin the main repeats on the way back.

THE PROPERTIES OF RIBBING

Where might you want to use rib? The obvious places are the cuffs of either socks or sleeves, or around the neckline or bottom hem of a jumper. In all of these cases, the ribbing is not necessarily just there for decoration.

One of the more useful properties of ribbing is how stretchy it is. More yarn is used in a section of ribbing than in the same number of stitches in stocking stitch. This is partly due to the fact that purl stitches—depending on the knitter—can take up a bit more yarn than knit stitches. The journey the yarn takes around the needle for a purl stitch is slightly longer than the journey it takes for a knit stitch. That's a technical conversation

best kept for another book, but the net result is that rib can really s-t-r-e-t-c-h.

To reduce the effect of this extra stretch, a pattern might suggest that the ribbed section at the hem or cuffs of a jumper, or round the brim of a hat should be worked with a slightly smaller needle than the one used for the rest of the project. There are times, however, when that extra bit of give is extremely useful, and you can use it to your advantage. Take the cuff of a sock, for example. People's calves tend to be wider at the top than at the bottom, and the top of a sock is where you find the cuff, so it's a good idea to make sure it fits there comfortably, without cutting into the wearer's leg.

It seems slightly odd to me, then, that most people seem to believe that ribbing draws the fabric in, when the exact opposite is true. If you look at a sock, in a relaxed, and unstretched state (the sock, not you), you'll see that the ribbed cuff does indeed look narrower than the sock's body. It's certainly true that the purl ditches in a piece of ribbing concertina in on themselves, contracting and collapsing the fabric along its horizontal plane.

Visually, then, the sock is indeed narrower here, but that doesn't mean it contains less fabric. Picture a curtain: you can pull it across the entire width of a window. You know that the window is a certain width, and you can assume that the curtain is actually even wider, as it has all of those lovely, undulating gathers. Very good. Now open the curtain, and the gathers get compressed, as they squeeze themselves together at the sides of the window. Although the curtain now takes up less horizontal space, you know for a fact that there it contains more than enough material to cover the total width of the window with plenty left over. See the parallel? This is no different.

So, although the sock cuff gathers in, there is still more fabric in it than if it had been knitted in stocking stitch.

Another reason to use ribbing in all the aforementioned places is the fact that it has no vertical curl. The vertical columns of knits and purls act like the boning in a vintage corset, keeping the fabric nice and straight. You don't want your socks rolling down, or your sleeves rolling up, unless you choose to wear them with a certain casual flair. Ending a sleeve or a sock with a few centimetres of ribbing mercifully prevents this from happening.

You might, of course, simply like the aesthetics of elegant parallel lines flowing up your work. And that, I think, is reason enough to use it.

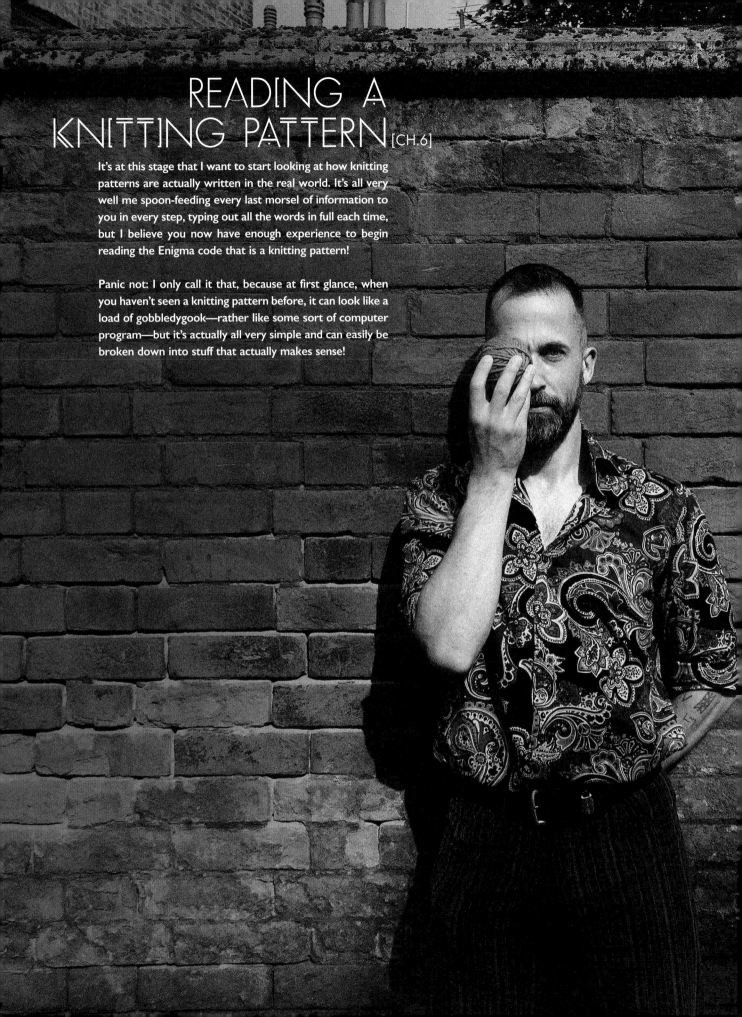

READING A
KNITTING PATTERN [CH.6]

It's at this stage that I want to start looking at how knitting patterns are actually written in the real world. It's all very well me spoon-feeding every last morsel of information to you in every step, typing out all the words in full each time, but I believe you now have enough experience to begin reading the Enigma code that is a knitting pattern!

Panic not: I only call it that, because at first glance, when you haven't seen a knitting pattern before, it can look like a load of gobbledygook—rather like some sort of computer program—but it's actually all very simple and can easily be broken down into stuff that actually makes sense!

You already know what RS and WS mean, so you are used to seeing some abbreviations, but here are some other standard ones:

K - KNIT

This is usually followed by a number, which refers to the number of stitches that you are supposed to knit before moving on to the next instruction. So 'K4' means 'knit four stitches'.

P - PURL

I reckon you can probably work this one out!
Yes, it's purl. Again, it's often followed by a number, so 'P10' would be an instruction to 'purl ten stitches'.

ST °R STS - STITCH °R STITCHES

This is a word that gets used a LOT in a knitting pattern, so you can save a lot of time and space by using an abbreve (sorry, couldn't resist!).

SL - SLIP

Can also take a number: 'SL1' or 'SL2'.

KW AND PW - KNITWISE & PURLWISE

We talked about these when learning about slipping stitches: knitwise and purlwise, sometimes written 'as if to knit' or 'as if to purl'. Usually refers to the direction that you insert the needle into the next stitch. (You may see combinations of the last two, such as 'SL1KW', which means that you are to 'slip one stitch knitwise'.)

That's about all the ones that we have discussed so far. I'll talk about any others as we get to them through the rest of the book.

Now that you know a little bit about how patterns are written, I can show you how the pattern for the 2x2 rib we've been talking about might be written out.

EXAMPLE 1:
Row 1 (RS): *K2, P2; repeat from * to end of row.
.
.
.   Repeat Row 1.
.
.
    Let's look at that in a bit more detail.

The asterisk at the start of the row denotes that what follows it is to be included in some kind of repeated figure.

Then you get the 'K2, P2' section. This is the meat of the repeat itself. You now know that it stands for 'knit two stitches, purl two stitches'.

The semi colon after the 'K2, P2' bit denotes the end of the repeated section, and finally there's an instruction that tells you what to repeat. All simple stuff, right?

Oddly, in this one situation, the instructions for working this type of ribbing in the round are *exactly the same,* except for replacing the word 'row' with the word 'round' each time! Lovely stuff...

You might, on the other hand, see the same pattern written out as follows:

EXAMPLE 2:
Row 1 (RS): [K2, P2] to end of row.
.
.
.   Repeat Row 1.
.   In this instance, the bit inside the square brackets is the

bit that you would repeat, and the rest of the line tells you to keep repeating it until the end of the row. Annoyingly, sometimes the square brackets might be curved brackets, or some other variation of what you see here, but usually, you'll be able to work out what it all means.

THE ANATOMY OF A STITCH [CH.7]

Knowing a bit about what a stitch actually looks like, and how it relates to the stitches to either side, above, and below, can really help with understanding what is going on in your knitting. Particularly so that we all know we're talking the same language later on.

If you look at a swatch of stocking stitch, you'll already be familiar with the fact that you can see all of the knit stitches on the right side of the fabric and all of the purl bumps, or purl stitches, on the wrong side.

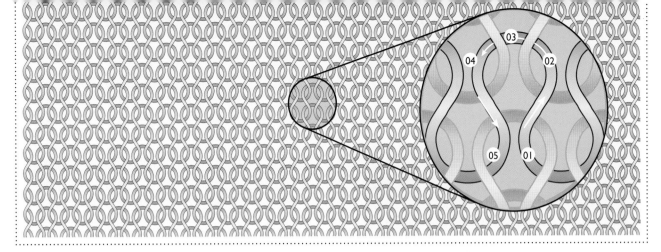

THE KNIT STITCH

Focusing just on the right side for now, have look at the diagram at the top of this page. All those lovely knit stitches look like little Vs, and boy, do they know how to please the obsessive in me by lining up nicely, side by side, and top to toe!

Knit stitches, or stocking stitch

Each 'V' is made up of two diagonal lines that splay apart at the top and come together at the bottom. We call these the 'legs' of the stitch. Each knit stitch has a 'right leg' and a 'left leg'. You can work out for yourself which is which…

Let's try to isolate just one, though, and look at it in a bit more detail, following the path of the yarn as it journeys through our chosen stitch. Refer to diagram at the top of the page.

The right leg, starting bottom centre (01), works its way diagonally upwards, and to the right. When it gets to the top, it disappears (02).

If you stretch the fabric a bit, you'll see that it goes behind *both* legs of the stitch above it (03), then emerges once more, becoming the top of the left leg (04). Finally, it works its way back down to the bottom, to the centre of the V, where it disappears once more (05).

So, although we call it a V (and it's really helpful to stick with that, as it's so pictorially representative), it's actually a loop, which I suppose should come as no surprise: when it was on the needle we were thinking about it as exactly that!

Now let's pretend that the stitch we've just been looking at is the green stitch in the diagram directly above this paragraph. Starting in the same place as before (marked 01 on both), let's follow our yarn in the *other* direction, and see where it comes from *before* becoming the right leg our green stitch.

From the bottom centre of the stitch in question (green) it disappears into the top centre of the stitch immediately below it (shown in blue). From there, it goes around the back of the right leg of the blue stitch, and around the back of the left leg of the stitch that sits one row, below and one column to the right of our main stitch. That's marked in red on the diagram. Next, it emerges from the top centre of the red stitch, as the bottom of the left leg of the stitch immediately to the right of our main stitch (marked in yellow).

Complicated as that might appear when written out in words, one stitch elegantly becomes the next, all the way along the row. The stitches from one row are all interlinked with the ones in the rows below and above. They are connected to each other in such a way that you simply cannot separate them without resorting to cutting the yarn. I'm sure there's a good metaphor for life in there somewhere.

Incidentally, it's this constant curving-back-on-itself shape that gives the knitted fabric its spring and stretch. (A single row looks a bit like a sine wave, with the tops and the bottoms of the wave squeezed up next to each other.)

THE PURL STITCH

Now I want you to turn your swatch over and look in more detail at what the *purl* stitches look like.

You are now looking at what appears to be a series of little horizontal bars of yarn, and the rows are grouped together in pairs. Each *pair* of rows has an upper row and a lower row, and one is offset from the other by the width of half a stitch.

Every one of the horizontal bars in the *upper* row of a pair was the top of the loop when it was a stitch on your needle. Call it the head of the loop, or whatever you like, but that's what it was, and that's how it ended up where it is now. The bars in the *lower* row of each pair are formed from that little bit of yarn that travels from one stitch to the next. Perhaps surprisingly, the yarn in one of these bars does not come from one single stitch. Half of it comes from the stitch to its left, and the other half from the stitch to its right. Don't forget, this is the back of what the knit stitches look like, and this lower bar relates to the bit on the front where the yarn goes through to the back of the fabric as it finishes being one stitch (and ending up right here), then emerges again, as the start of the next. Make sense?

Comparing what's going on here with what we saw when we looked at the right side of the swatch, the head of each loop (or to put it another way, each bump in the upper row of a pair) is made from the bit of yarn that runs from the top of the right

leg of a knit stitch to the top of the left leg of the same stitch. When the yarn disappears through to the back of the fabric (marked 02 on the diagram at the top of the last page), *this* is where it comes out: it becomes an upper-row purl bump on the wrong side.

That's all well and good, and very useful stuff to know. Things look a little different, however, when you are dealing with the loops of yarn that are currently on your needle.

Staying with the purl side of our swatch for a moment, take a look at the loops that are still on your needle. Immediately below them, there is a purl bump: what we *now* know to be the head of the stitch in the row below. It looks like the stitch that is still on the needle is wearing a little collar.

Every time you see a stitch with such a 'collar', you'll know that you are looking at a purl stitch. Turn the swatch over, or refer back to the photos on the previous page, and there aren't any collars around the stitches on this side. That's because you are looking at knit stitches.

Remember, therefore: 'collar = I'm about to work into a purl stitch', and 'no collar = I'm about to work into a knit stitch'. This is crucial knowledge for being able to 'read' your knitting.

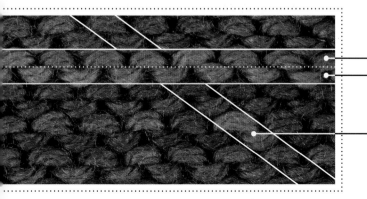

Upper Row
Lower Row

Half-stitch offset

READING Y°UR KNITTING
Whuh?

That's right, 'reading' your knitting. It's a very useful skill.

It means being able to look at a piece of knitted fabric and understand how it was made.

More useful still, it's the ability to pick up your half-finished project, after what might only be a few hours, but could just as easily be days, weeks or even months, and know *exactly* what row of the pattern you are supposed to be on, and what stitch needs to come next.

There are actually lots of different elements to the art of reading your knitting, drawing on certain aspects of clairvoyance and necromancy—no wait… That can't be right. I think I meant looking and counting. I get them confused.

Either way, I'll try to distil this handy talent into useful sections here.

COUNTING: H°W MANY STITCHES?
One fundamental aspect of reading your knitting is knowing how to count your stitches.

Um, I think I know how to count, Nathan, I'm not a two-year-old!

That's as may be, but knitted stitches can be really tiny, and the bits you need to count might not be the bits you think they are. It's just not a good idea to risk working on something that is entirely based on precise numbers, if there's a chance that your numbers might be off by a stitch or two here and there. Knitting requires a much higher level of precision than you might imagine.

As long as the stitches that need counting are still on the needles, counting them is a piece of cake. You simply count the loops of yarn. One loop equals one stitch. They are right there in front of you, and there's not much that can go wrong.

Once those stitches are no longer on the needle, you might find that you need to count the stitches in a row some way down—well *that's* a yarn of a totally different fibre! Different, yes, but now that you know about the anatomy of a stitch, it should be easy as pie.

Another cake reference.

That's a yarn cake, of course. (And the joke there is that yarn can come to you in the form of a ball, a skein… or a cake!)

When counting *knit* stitches below the needles, simply look for the Vs. If you look at your knitting in slightly the wrong way, your eye will instead want to see things that look like lots of capital As without their crossbar.

V - Correct
A - Incorrect

That's not the right way of looking at them though, as you would be grouping together the left-hand leg of one stitch with the right-hand leg of another. This can really skew your numbers, so make sure you were always counting Vs, not As. Just count them across the row, taking care, of course, not to skip from one row to another along the way.

On the purl side, you need to look for the bumps that make up the *upper* row of a grouped pair of rows. Counting the *lower* bumps will give you the same discrepancies as trying to count the crossbar-less As on the other side.

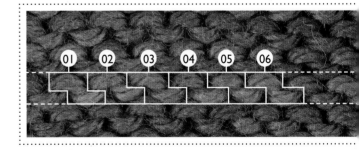

Counting stitches in knitting is a notoriously tricky thing to do. You sometimes need to use a bit of licence and guesswork as you go along. I've found a few tips along the way that have really helped me, and I hope they'll help you too.

- Count your stitches at least twice, but preferably *thrice* (just because a word is archaic, doesn't mean I can't use it). You'll be amazed at just how often a recount gives you a different result. A third count *should* corroborate one or other of your first two attempts. (Obviously, if your second count returns the same number as your original count, you can probably assume you're good to go.)

- DON'T BLINK! I know that sounds really stupid, but as your eye is merrily moving along the row, in the length of time it takes to blink, it will have skipped ahead a tiny fraction, and when your eyes reopen, your brain gets disorientated. At least, *mine* does. The amount of times I've lost count part of the way through a row count, only to realise it happened immediately after a blink, convinces me that the two things are definitely related.

If you absolutely *must* blink mid-row, get to a nice round number, e.g. 50 stitches, then stop counting and hold your thumbnail at the point you just reached. *Then* you can blink, safe in the knowledge that when your eyes open again you have the position of your thumbnail for reference and can carry on counting, until such time as you need to blink again. Trust me, I promise it's a thing!

Sometimes, you will be required to count stitches along a row that is composed of combinations of different stitches, but you should be able to adapt these methods to whatever situation you find yourself in, without too much trouble.

Counting rib stitches is a doddle, by the way. If you are working 2x2 rib, for example, you know that the pattern repeat is four stitches, so you can simply count the purl ditches, and multiply the number by four. It's rather like the quickest way to know how many sheep there are in a field*.

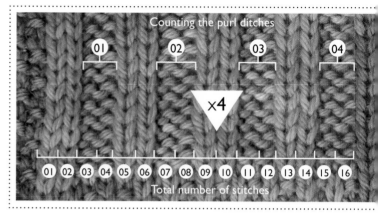

It's the same formula for 2x1 rib, or any other rib for that matter: you still count the purl ditches, but multiply by the number of stitches in one repeat, and your work is done.

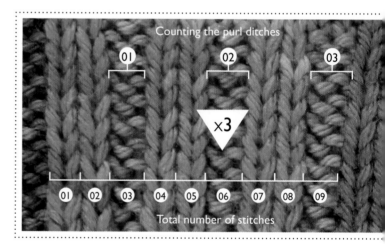

*Count the total number of legs, and divide by four.

GL°SSARY

COUNTING: H°W MANY R°WS?

Counting how many rows you have worked can be just as tricky, if not trickier, than counting the number of stitches *along* a row. Obviously, you are now working vertically, rather than horizontally, but there's a bit more to it than that.

Good news: with knit stitches, you can still look for the Vs. They all fit into each other very nicely, like a wedding party in the early 90s, doing the official dance to The Gap Band's *Ooops Upside Your Head*. The knits, then, are easy to count. The mental picture I've just given you, however, is quite difficult to erase.

It's those perishing purls that you have to watch out for! The fact that the bumps in the lower row of each grouped pair are offset by half a stitch each time, means your eye can easily be dragged off course, and you end up counting a *diagonal* line of stitches, rather than a straight column. This can produce some very irregular results indeed.

Remember that purl stitches are defined only by the bumps along the *upper* row of each grouped pair. It's important that you ONLY count these upper-row bumps as you work your way up.

I find it useful to catch the point of one of my knitting needles under each relevant purl bump as I count upwards. That way, if my eye gets lost, I've always got the needle tip holding my place for reference.

READING M°RE C°MPLICATED KNITTING

Once you learn some of the more involved techniques in knitting, beyond knits and purls, e.g. lacework or cables, you'll find that reading your knitting becomes an even *more* valuable skill. Sadly, that's just when it gets a little more complicated.

My advice is simply this: every time you learn a new stitch, practise it a few times, then examine it closely. Stretch the fabric apart and *really* focus on what the new element looks like. Where do the strands of yarn go? What shape does it remind you of?

The key is to get so familiar with it that you'll properly *own* what you are doing, understanding it from the inside, rather than just blindly following instructions.

Then, when you need to read your knitting in the future, you'll totally be able to spot key elements at a glance: you'll see a particular confluence of yarn strands, and be able to say to yourself, *'That's a K2tog*, I know* I did one of those on Row 14 of the repeat, and it was 16 stitches before the end of the row. *That* means I must be HERE!' You will then be able to pick up where you left off with confidence, knowing you are in the right place to carry on.

**Don't panic: you haven't missed anything—
we haven't covered 'K2tog' yet—that's coming up next...*

FURTHER
HⁿW TⁿS [CH.8]

t's all very well learning about different combinations
of knit and purl stitches, and how they come together
to make the different textures we've been looking at so
far, but there's a whole lot more to knitting than that.

t's time to focus on the stuff that will take your knitting
to the next level.

This chapter looks at decreases (taking stitches away
from the number you started with), and increases
(adding more stitches to your knitting), which are not
only ways of making knitted items in different shapes,
rather than the plain old squares and rectangles you've
become used to, but they are also the building blocks of
lace knitting. Very useful knowledge indeed!

We'll also be looking at cables, but I'll explain more
about what they are when we get to that bit.

DECREASES AND INCREASES

Unless you are happy knitting rectangles and squares for the rest of your life, you are probably going to want to know how to decrease or increase your stitch count during a project. Put simply, the more stitches you have, the wider your knitting will be, and the fewer stitches you have, the narrower it will be.

Most things you make will be made to fit some part of the human body or other, and unless you live in the world of Minecraft, the likelihood is that you are not made up of squares!

Being able to create extra stitches, or get rid of unwanted stitches at will, gives you the opportunity to make pieces of knitted fabric in whatever shapes you need to fit the rather complex body shapes we often have to cover. Just take a look at your foot…

Decreases and increases don't just need to be used for *shaping* your knitting, however. Pairing an increase and a decrease won't necessarily change your stitch count, so the width of your work will stay the same, but in doing so, you can create an entirely new world of different patterns and textures, unlike anything you'll have done so far. That's is the basis of what is called lace knitting (the name usually given to any kind of knitting with lots of holes in it). You'll be amazed at how different your work can look just by employing some of these simple techniques.

DECREASES

Let's start with decreases. If you need to reduce your stitch count (either because you have just worked an increase and need to balance that with getting rid of an extra stitch, or because you want to make your knitting narrower), you'll want to work a decrease.

STUFF T° KN°W

Most decreases will 'lean' either to the left or to the right. For that reason, they are often referred to as 'left-leaning decreases' or 'right-leaning decreases'. (Some decreases don't lean either way, and good luck to them, but they can have their *own* box!)

Building up a column of, say, right-leaning decreases gives you a very smart, tidy line of stitches that slants towards the right. This line can make for a really useful feature, used decoratively, or to disguise the fact that there is anything as mundane as stitch reduction happening, or simply to create a striking visual feature in the design.

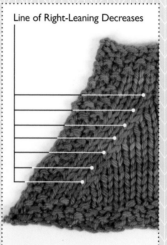
Line of Right-Leaning Decreases

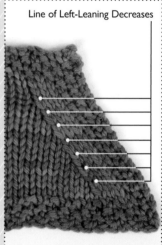
Line of Left-Leaning Decreases

The 'lean' is caused by the fact that the stitches have to stack on top of each other in one way or another. In a decrease that reduces two stitches into one, you will be pulling the loop of the new stitch through not one, as you usually do, but through *two* existing stitches. One of those stitches will necessarily end up sitting behind the other one, as they both try to occupy the space of a single stitch.

But if *both* stitches are sloping inwards, why is there a lean one way or the other? Well, the direction of the lean is governed by whichever of the two stitches ends up sitting on the top. Isn't that always the way?

The rule is this: if the rightmost (if there are only two stitches, shouldn't it be 'rightmore' as a comparative, as 'rightmost' is most definitely a superlative, only to be used with more than two items being compared…) stitch sits on top of the leftmost* one, the decrease will lean to the left, and if the leftmost stitch sits on top of the rightmost one, the decrease will lean to the right.

It gets a little more complicated with decreases involving larger numbers of stitches, because bigger numbers mean more combinations of position, but we'll cover those a bit further on.

Don't think it's not on its way…

SINGLE DECREASES

Single decreases decrease two stitches into one. The 'single' part of the name comes from the fact that you have reduced your stitch count by one stitch. These decreases are also called 'two-stitches-into-one' or 'one-stitch' or 'two to one' decreases. You are bound to end up using them more than any other kind, so let's get on with it!

K2T°G

The simplest decrease in the whole world just happens to be a right-leaning one. It is made by knitting two stitches together, and is called… wait for it… 'knit two together!' You'll often see that abbreviated to 'K2tog'. Here's how:

SCAN T° WATCH
MY K2T°G VID

STEP 1

Instead of inserting the tip of the right needle into the *first* stitch on the left needle, as if to do an ordinary knit stitch, here, you go into the *second* stitch on the left needle (the one that is to the left of the normal one), *as well as the first stitch*. To clarify, the right needle tip goes into two stitches at the same time.

STEP 2

Wrap the working yarn around the right needle tip as normal.

STEP 3

Draw a new loop of yarn through both original stitches, just like with a normal knit stitch, but take care not to lose either of them as you pass the needle tip through: it's important that the new loop goes through both of the old stitches.

STEP 4

Drop both of the old loops off the left needle tip, exactly like the last stage of a knit stitch, except that there are two loops to deal with, rather than just one.

This decrease is aptly named. It feels exactly like you are doing an ordinary knit stitch, it's just that you are working into two stitches instead of one. You are *literally* knitting two stitches together.

Remember my advice in the 'Reading Your Knitting' section (see page 83)? Now is a good time to put that into practice. I want you to inspect closely the decrease you've just made. First, count the number of stitches remaining on your needle. Assuming you knew how many you had to start with(!), you should now have one fewer than before. That's your decrease.

Second, look in detail at the decrease itself, and you'll see that one of the two stitches (the rightmore one—yes, I'm going with it!) has tucked itself behind the other (the leftmore one—you must've seen it coming: that one works for me as well). The leftmore stitch is slanting towards the right, and, being more visible for being the one on the top, it's *this* stitch that gives the decrease its 'lean'. In this case, of course, it's the right-facing lean I was talking about before.

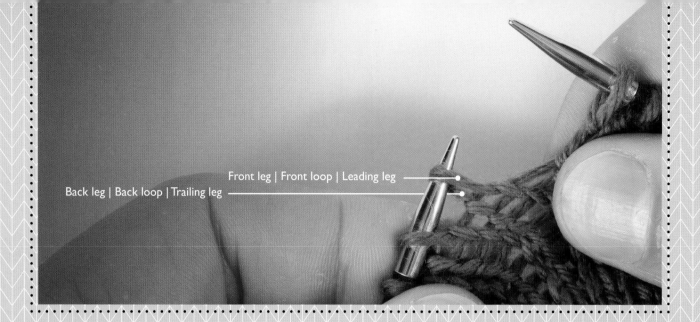

Front leg | Front loop | Leading leg

Back leg | Back loop | Trailing leg

A LITTLE KNIT NERDISM

I just want to butt in on my own chapter here, if I may—and who's going to stop me: it's my book?—to talk about twisted stitches, what causes them, and more importantly, what doesn't.

It's all about stitch mount. So many things are. Stitch mount is the term used to describe the way a stitch sits on the needle: how it is 'mounted'.

Each stitch has two 'legs'—a left leg and a right one, and the stitch will always have one leg in front of the needle, and one behind it (otherwise, it wouldn't be on the needle at all!). The right leg might be the one in front of the needle, in which case the left leg will be behind it, but it could just as easily be the other way round, and often is.

One problem in all of this is the sheer number of terms that exist to describe this stuff. In the picture above, the right leg might be called the 'front leg', because it is in front of the needle, or the 'front loop' (which is frankly, quite ridiculous when you come to think about it, as it is very obviously only part of a loop. Don't start. I hate it. It makes no sense to me either!).

Or, you just might send yourself straight to the top of my Christmas-card list, and refer to it as the 'leading leg' of the stitch.

(The leading leg of a stitch is the one that sits nearer to the tip of the needle.)

The left leg of the same stitch, in our picture above, might be called the 'back leg, the 'back loop' (ugh!), or the 'trailing' leg, meaning the leg that is further away from the needle tip.

I prefer to say 'leading leg' and 'trailing leg', for reasons that are about to become clear.

Usually, in an untwisted, or 'open' stitch, one leg stays over on one side of the stitch, and the other leg stays on the other, like boys and girls at a school dance. With twisted stitches, on the other hand, one of the legs crosses over the top of the other*. Whenever I look at twisted stitches, sitting there with their legs crossed, I always think they look desperate for a pee!

The twist makes the stitch a little bit more compact, and and as a result, it can look neater in some placements than its open-legged brothers.

So how do you achieve this twist?

Ask most knitters, and they will tell you that 'knitting through the back loop' twists the stitch, or that 'wrapping your yarn in the opposite direction when you create the stitch' will twist it. I hereby, and contentiously state, without any doubt in my mind, that I don't care how many times you hear one or both of these statements, they are in fact, entirely untrue.

The second one is never true, and although the first one may be true in some situations, it is very definitely not true in others, so can't be posited as a fact.

What these well-intentioned knitters actually mean, is that these actions *remount* the stitch on the needle. And what *that* means, is that if the leading leg of the stitch had been in front of the needle to begin with, it will now be behind it, and if the leading leg of the stitch had started off behind the needle, it will end up in front.

Twisted stitch, crossed legs

So what difference does it make if people say 'remount' or 'twist'?

Quite a lot.

The truth is that the only thing that dictates whether you end up with a twisted stitch or an open one is whether you work that stitch through the leading leg or through the trailing leg. Regardless of whether you are knitting or purling, regardless of how the stitch might be mounted on the needle, IT IS A UNIVERSAL TRUTH that if you work that stitch through the leading leg, you will end up with an open stitch, and if you work it through the trailing leg, it will be twisted.

Fact. End of. Finito. Prove me wrong, I dare you!!

I won't be able to change the way everyone thinks or speaks about this, no matter how frustrating it is to hear people saying things that are simply untrue, as if they were fact, but I'll just have to learn to build myself a bridge, and get over it!

Well, that was better out than in. Let's get back to the decreases.

Like boys and girls AFTER the school dance...

SSK

The corresponding symmetrical decrease to the K2tog is called the SSK. The letters stand for 'slip, slip, knit', which describes the process of creating this particular example of a single, left-leaning decrease. There are a few more steps in the process of performing the SSK than there are with the K2tog. Boo hoo. Deal with it.

Drum roll: here it comes:

SCAN T° WATCH
MY 'SSK' VID

STEP 1
Slip one stitch, knitwise (KW), from the left needle to the right.

STEP 2
Slip a second stitch, also KW from the left needle to the right.

STEP 3

Slip both stitches (together or individually—it doesn't matter for this step), this time purlwise, from the right needle, back to the left.

STEP 4

Insert the tip of the right needle into the first TWO stitches on the left needle, going in as if to knit them together through the back loops.

STEP 5

Wrap your yarn as normal.

STEP 6

Draw the new loop of yarn through the two stitches.

STEP 7

Drop both original stitches off the tip of the right needle.

Again, I want you to look closely at the stitch you have just made. Just as before, you *should* have one stitch fewer than you started with, but this time you will see that the decrease is leaning to the left, because this time it's the rightmore stitch that is lying over the top of the leftmore one. (And no: I'm not letting that one go!)

Why all that slipping around at the start? That's important because we want to create a mirror image decrease to the K2tog, and in order to correctly achieve that mirror symmetry, we need to set up a couple of things, before doing the step that actually decreases the stitch count.

Firstly, the K2tog is worked with the stitches mounted on the needle with the leading leg in front of it. Mirroring that in the right way means that for the SSK, we need to have the stitches mounted with the leading leg behind the needle, and the trailing leg in front of it, and all that slipping around is what will sort that out for us.

Slipping the stitches knitwise over to the right needle mounts them how we want them, but leaves them on the wrong needle. They need to be transferred back to the left needle, then, and we do it purlwise because we've already remounted them, and don't want to change that as we move them back.

Once the stitches are mounted the right way, because both decreases end up as open stitches, we know they must both be worked through the leading leg. We know that the leading leg of the K2tog is at the front, and because we've just remounted these stitches, meaning the leading leg is at the back, it suddenly makes perfect sense that the decrease in an SSK is worked through eye back loops. Logic, and a little bit of creative thinking tells us so.

You can actually combine Steps 3 and 4, saving yourself quite a lot of time and effort. Let's call this new bit 'Step 3a':

STEP 3A

Insert the tip of the LEFT needle into the first two stitches on the right needle, as if to purl them both together. That means going in through the front loops of *both* stitches, from back to front, and from right to left. Ignoring Step 4 completely, you can now move right along to Step 5, collecting your £200 en route. Dandy.

You could, of course—and some dreadful people do—simply bypass all that slipping malarkey, and just knit the two stitches together through the back loops. You'll still get a decrease, and yes, it will still lean to the left, which might very well be enough to keep you perfectly happy. But those two stitches will be lying with their legs crossed, creating a small bump in the surface of your work. If the thought of that doesn't give you any trouble, then good luck to you, but personally, I'm an absolute stickler for symmetry and perfection when to comes to my knitting. I'm even *more* particular when it comes to the selection of what decreases I will pair together. When you are investing this much time and energy into knitting something, I absolutely believe that it's utterly worth taking a little *extra* care, so that your knitting can be as close to perfect as it is possible to be.

SINGLE PURL DECREASES

It's quite possible to work purl versions of the left- and right-leaning single decreases as well. You might want to hide a decrease in the purl texture on your right side, or perhaps you

need to perform a decrease on the wrong side of your work. It could be one of any number of reasons: most likely one you couldn't possibly have thought of yet. There it is, staring you right in the face, sniggering ever-so slightly. Forewarned is forearmed and all that, so it's good to know a little bit about purl increases, *just in case…*

P2T°G

The purl equivalent of the K2tog, not surprisingly, is the P2tog. In much the same way that a K2tog is essentially the same as a normal knit stitch, except that the tip of the right needle goes into *two* stitches at the same time, the P2tog is likewise essentially the same as a normal purl stitch, with the same exception: the tip of the right needle goes through the first two stitches on the left needle instead of just one.

Here, very briefly then, are the steps for the P2tog:

SCAN T° WATCH MY 'P2T°G' VID

STEP 1

Insert the tip of the right needle into the first two stitches on the left needle, going in purlwise.

STEP 2

Complete the manoeuvre by wrapping the yarn and drawing the new loop through the two stitches, before dropping them off the left needle. Not much to it, really… (There's also not a single picture in the world that can illustrate all of those things in one go, so I thought you might enjoy this picture of a hammerhead shark instead. Weird, aren't they?)

SSP

The SSP (slip, slip, purl) is the logical purl equivalent of the SSK, but unfortunately it's a bit less straightforward, so I certainly wouldn't expect you to work out how it is done for yourself. Also, it contains one particular manoeuvre that rather gives one the feeling that certain soft, round parts of one's anatomy might be in mortal danger. Despite all of that, I'm still a fan!

The steps are these:

SCAN T° WATCH
MY 'SSP' VID

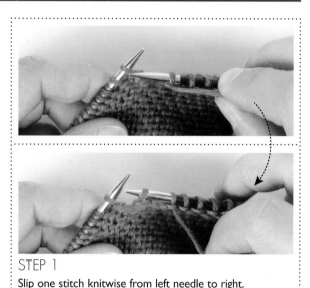

STEP 1
Slip one stitch knitwise from left needle to right.

STEP 2
Slip a second stitch knitwise from left needle to right.

STEP 3
Slip both of those stitches, this time purlwise, back from the right needle to the left. It doesn't matter if you slip them individually or both together. Just like the start of the SSK, these three steps remount the stitches, so that even when that famously generously proportioned singer has screeched her final squawk, the surface of our knitting will still be smooth, and not subject to the kind of irritating bumps that a couple of cross-legged stitches would so enthusiastically provide. By that, I mean the decrease will still be good and flat, once you've completed all the steps.

STEP 4
This is where the mortal peril comes into play.
Insert the tip of the right needle into the first two stitches on the left needle, but unlike any time so far, you have to go into them both *as if to purl them through the back loops*. Don't freak out: it really is THE most unintuitive way to enter a stitch (or in this case, two), and it will feel totally wrong, but trust me, it's correct.

You have to take the tip of the right needle ALL THE WAY round the back of the two stitches in question and go into them from the back to the front, and from the left-hand side to the right. Every single time I purl a stitch through the back loop, it always feels like I'm about to stab myself in the eye with my own knitting needle. Why, what anatomical parts did you think I meant?

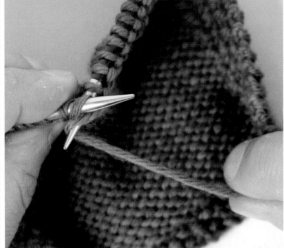

STEP 5

Now you can wrap the yarn around the tip of the right needle, just like a normal purl stitch.

STEP 6

This is another bit that perhaps needs a bit more care than you might expect: you still draw the new loop of yarn back through the two stitches, but because of the unusual angle, just make sure you exit *both* of the stitches completely, as it's quite easy to miss one of them, and you probably won't notice until sometime later, as much of what takes place during this step goes on around the back of the work, where you can't really see it. After that's gone well you're good to carry on, and drop the two original stitches off the left needle as normal.

In a bed of purl stitches (a texture sometimes referred to as 'reverse stocking stitch'), it's not easy to see any kind of lean on these decreases. It is there, but it's actually much more visible on the other side of the work. Useful if you need to work a decrease on the wrong side of your work, but you want the lean to show up on the right side.

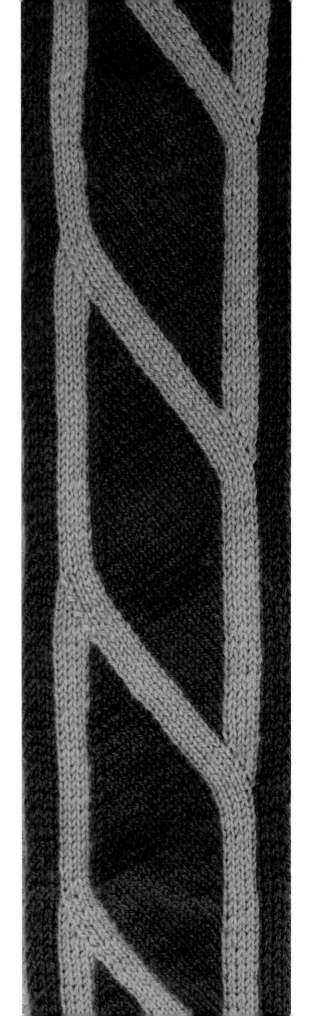

DOUBLE DECREASES

You're way ahead of me: double decreases reduce your stitch count by two stitches, magically turning three stitches into just one.

Unlike single decreases, where there are really only two options—one stitch can lie either under or over the other—when you are dealing with three stitches there are suddenly many more options regarding how those stitches will be arranged when they reach their final destination.

STACKED DOUBLE DECREASES

The simplest examples of a double decrease are what I call 'stacked decreases'. (I would advise using the term with caution: I'm not altogether sure that anyone else uses it, and I might have made it up.) This group of decreases comprises the K3tog (knit *three* together) and the SSSK (slip, slip, *slip*, knit).

In both, the three stitches end up stacked on top of each other, with the first on top of the second, which in turn lies on top of the third.

They are actually made in exactly the same ways as their single-decrease counterparts, but just in case you can't picture how that works, here come the instructions:

K3TOG

The K3tog leans to the right, just like its two-stitch counterpart, the only real difference is that you are working with three stitches instead of two.

SCAN TO WATCH
MY 'K3TOG' VID

STEP 1

Instead of inserting the tip of the right needle into the first *two* stitches on the left needle, as in the K2tog, here you will go into the first *three* stitches on the left needle, knitwise of course, so that your right needle tip has gone into all three stitches together. You knew that.

STEP 2

Wrap the working yarn around the right needle tip as normal.

STEP 3

Draw a new loop yarn through the three old stitches, just as expected.

STEP 4

Drop all three of the old loops off the left needle tip, exactly like the last stage of a K2tog, except that there are three loops to contend with, rather than just two.

SSSK

Not a great deal to add here. You could probably write this paragraph yourself based on what you now know about the K3tog. You know, three stitches, same as two, yada, yada, yada…

SCAN T° WATCH
MY 'SSSK' VID

STEP 1

Slip three stitches, ONE AT A TIME, knitwise, from the left needle to the right.

STEP 2

Slip all three stitches (together or individually—it doesn't matter), *purlwise* this time, from the right needle, back to the left.

STEP 3

Insert the tip of the right needle, as if to knit through the back loops (that's going in from front to back, and from right to left), into the first THREE stitches on the left needle.

STEP 4

Wrap your yarn as normal.

STEP 5

Draw the new loop of yarn through all three of the original stitches.

STEP 6

Drop all three original stitches off the tip of the right needle. Have a close look at both of these decreases once you have completed them. You'll see how the stitches stack up on top of each other, looking rather like a short section of a very tiny spiral staircase. The lean is pretty evident.

STACKED DºUBLE PURL DECREASES

The P3tog (purl *three* together) and the SSSP (slip, slip, *slip*, purl) are created in exactly the same way as their single-decrease counterparts, so this time I'm not going to bother with the steps. Call it creative autonomous learning—or: *work it out your bloody self!*

ºTHER LEFT- AND RIGHT-LEANING DºUBLE DECREASES

There *might* come a time when you find you want to decrease three stitches into one in a way that sends the centre stitch to the back and lets the two outside stitches cross over in front.

Such decreases are entirely possible, and there is a left-leaning version as well as a right-leaning one. In the interests of brevity, however (who shouted, 'too late!'?), I'll keep those for Book 2…

THE CENTRED DºUBLE DECREASE (CDD)

The last decrease I want to talk about here is probably my favourite! (That doesn't mean it's the one I would choose to use most often—heavens no! I always choose the most appropriate decrease for the job in hand, based not on personal preference but on what I need the decrease to achieve. All that aside, though, it has to be said, I am rather fond of this one for reasons of aesthetics, as well as practicality. It's win-win.)

Once again, it's a three-stitches-into-one decrease, and as such, reduces your stitch count by a total of two stitches.

The difference with *this* one is that it doesn't lean to the left or to the right, but rather smugly, it appears to sit perfectly symmetrically on your knitting. If you build a column of CDDs in your work, it looks like a very prominent vertical ridge of knit stitches, standing proud from the rest of the work. Gotta love a bit of symmetry! That's the old CDO rumbling away at me again.

The steps are still nice and simple, but there's a new one to watch out for: for *this* decrease, you pass TWO stitches TOGETHER over the third, rather than just passing one stitch over another, as you have done until now.

SCAN Tº WATCH
MY 'CDD' VID

STEP 1

Slip 2 sts TOGETHER, and KNITWISE, from the left needle to the right. (To remind you, insert the tip of the right needle into the first two stitches on the left needle, as if you were about to do a K2tog.)

STEP 2

Knit the next st from the left needle.

STEP 3

Insert the tip of the left needle into the front of both the SECOND and THIRD stitches on the right needle, then pass them both together over the first stitch, and drop them off the needle to complete the move.

Column of CDDs, worked on every other row.

You won't really get the full impact of the punch that this decrease can pack unless and until you have worked a few more rows, stacking several CDDs on top of each other. Then you'll understand why I like it so much. I'm tempted to say it feels like a very masculine sort of decrease (see above).

NB: To create the bold, perhaps rather phallic, statement of the vertical line of CDDs that I keep harping on about, you would only ever work this decrease on every other row. If you are working in stocking stitch, you would simply purl the WS rows, saving the CDD for each RS row.

ALL THAT GLISTERS

It should be pointed out here that the CDD isn't in fact totally symmetrical, the way most people will tell you it is. I hate to say it, but they are wrong. It looks symmetrical, sure enough, but I'm sorry to break it to you: it's a charlatan, a scoundrel, a rapscallion, if you will.

It's true that the centre stitch does stand very vertically, and does not lean to the left or the right, but here begins its rascally deception. That centre stitch, so proud and gallant, hides a dirty, and yes, I'll say it: unsymmetrical little secret!

I know. Shocking.

Behind that centre stitch, the other two stitches necessarily have to cross one on top of the other, and that, as we know, is what gives a decrease a lean. You don't really see the lean in this case because the centre stitch is hiding the lie, but it's a lie nonetheless. (If you are interested in these things, it's the new rightmore stitch that sits over the top of the new leftmore one, meaning that the invisible treachery is actually leaning towards the left.)

But if it looks like a symmetrical decrease, why does it matter that it's not?

A good question. Ultimately, it doesn't matter a jot. Not a wit. But I'm supposed to be telling you the facts about knitting, and I want you to be able to trust me. If I said something that wasn't actually true, and you ever found this out for yourself, you'd be perfectly justified in never believing anything I say ever again! (Also, let's be honest, I'm also sharing this with you so that you can be smug about it in conversation with other knitters who, likely as not, won't know anything about this most dastardly of knitting cover-ups…)

And with total openness at heart, I should tell you that there is another way of working the CDD, and it's one that I've devised myself. No tutorial needed: just follow the instructions for the SSK, but in Step 1, slip TWO stitches (TOGETHER and KNITWISE) instead of one, and in Step 4, you'll be going into three stitches, instead of two. Ta-da! You're very welcome.

If you come across a decrease in a pattern that hasn't been covered in this chapter, nine times out of ten, the designer will be aware that it is a little out of the ordinary, and will no doubt have included instructions detailing how it should be done, so I think you're good to move on.

INCREASES

As the name suggests, these stitches *increase* your stitch count. Unsurprisingly, there are many different increases, and they all have their places in different circumstances. Some are decorative, and you may want to use them as a specific feature in your work, and some are a little less visible. (I hate to say it, but there aren't any that are *completely* invisible, particularly if you are working with stocking stitch, the uniformity which is so easily broken up. It's a lot easier to hide decreases and increases in the textures of reverse stocking stitch or garter stitch.)

YARN°VERS

This is the easiest type of single increase out there. It increases your stitch count by a total of one stitch, and it's also one of the most visible, leaving a very prominent hole, or eyelet, in your knitting.

Standard Yarnover

DISCLAIMER

You will see 'yarn over' as often as 'yarnover' in the knitting world. It seems to be a matter of preference. I personally use the compound noun, 'yarnover', when I am talking about the stitch you are about to learn. I do it to differentiate between the increase and any other usage, such as in the sentence, 'take the yarn over the top of the left needle', where it definitely needs to be two separate words. So, for this book, 'yarnover' (abbreviated to YO) it is.

The yarnover is the basis of most lace knitting techniques. Pairing yarnovers with decreases keeps the stitch count consistent and can give you patterns of lacy holes and sloping lines: in this way you can basically paint pictures on the fabric of your knitting. The yarnover is not just for lace, however, and you'll see it used wherever you want an increase and either actively want, or at least don't mind, the appearance of an eyelet.

Although the steps for making a YO on the RS of stocking stitch and on the RS of reverse stocking stitch are actually exactly the same, they feel a little different in the execution, so let's look at them separately.

SCAN T° WATCH MY 'YARN°VERS IN B°TH ST°CKING STITCH AND REVERSE ST°CKING STITCH' VID.

YARN°VERS IN ST°CKING STITCH

STEP 1

Work to where you want your YO hole to appear. As the previous stitch was a knit stitch, your working yarn will be at the back of the work.

STEP 2

Bring the working yarn to the front of the work, between the two needle tips.

STEP 3

Now take the working yarn to the back of the work, but take it over the top of the right needle. Your working yarn is now at the back of the work, ready to continue knitting.

YARN°VERS IN REVERSE ST°CKING STITCH

STEP 1

Work to the point where you want your YO to appear. This time, the last stitch you made was a purl stitch, so your working yarn will be at the front of the work.

STEP 2

Take the working yarn to the back of the work, by laying it over the top of the right needle.

STEP 3

Now bring the working yarn to the front, this time coming between the two needle tips. Your working yarn is now at the front of the work once more, ready to continue purling.

In both of these cases, the working yarn has made one complete revolution around the right needle tip. The only difference is that it started and ended at the back of the work for stocking stitch, and it started and ended its journey at the front of the work for reverse stocking stitch.

Again, in both, you will notice that the working yarn has travelled around the right needle in an anticlockwise direction, as seen from looking down at the tip of the needle. This is the same direction that you would normally wrap the yarn when either knitting or purling. This is not a coincidence. It is so that the extra loop of yarn created by the yarnover sits on the right needle orientated in the correct way.

You won't really see the hole in your knitting yet. Only once you have worked a row over the top of the row that contains the YO will the hole really become apparent. When you get back to the YO, on the following row or round, you will just knit or purl into it as directed by your pattern, as though it were any ordinary stitch. It will look and feel a little different from the stitches that you are used to working into, as it doesn't have the same structure as an ordinary stitch, but just treat it in exactly the same manner.

I have to admit, I was a little bit allergic to YOs when I first started knitting. I really wasn't into lace knitting: I think it was a guy thing. I was only really interested in knitting things that I would want to wear, and lacy holes seemed way too girly for me. I was also such a fan of the uniformity of knitted stitches, and didn't like breaking that up with little holes everywhere. It took me a long time to learn to embrace the YO for the useful

and decorative increase I now know it to be. (Experimenting with lace knitting using thick, chunky, and dare I say, manly yarn really helped with that—it turns out lace doesn't have to be girly at all. Hoodathunkit?)

TWISTED YARN°VERS
If you find that the holes created by a YO are a little larger than you would like them to be, you can reduce the size of them on the row or round that follows the one where the yarnover was created.

Twisted Yarnover

A twisted YO is created in exactly the same way as those described above, but when you return to the YO on the following row, instead of working into the YO loop in the normal way—i.e. through the front loop—you knit or purl into the YO through the back loop. This will cross the legs of the stitch, drawing the two sides of the YO hole closer together, and the gap will close up quite a lot. There will still be a hole, but it won't be as large as a standard YO eyelet.

MAKE ºNE RIGHT & MAKE ºNE LEFT

If you don't want holes in your work at all, the Make One Right (M1R) and Make One Left (M1L) increases are probably your best option. These are the increases I tend to use most often.

I find them to be as close to invisible as possible, although I should add that some people find other types of increase are less prominent in their work.

Knitters are individual beasts.

Like the K2tog and the SSK decrease, the M1R and M1L increases lean to the right and left respectively. This is worth bearing in mind when placing increases in your knitting, as one may be more effective in a certain position than the other.

Both of these increases create the extra stitch from the little stretch of yarn that runs between the last stitch worked (now on your right needle) and the next stitch *to be worked* (still on the left needle). This bit of yarn is often referred to as the 'running yarn' because it 'runs' from one stitch to the next.

Here, then, are the steps for both:

MAKE ºNE RIGHT (M1R): RIGHT-LEANING

SCAN Tº WATCH
MY 'M1R' VID

STEP 1
Insert the tip of the left needle under the running yarn, going in from back to front, and lift it up onto the left needle. (You may find it easier to lift the yarn with the right needle first, then put the left needle tip in underneath it, going in under the yarn from back to front.)

STEP 2
Knit into this new stitch THROUGH THE FRONT LOOP.

It will feel more intuitive to knit into the back loop rather than the front, as it's the back loop that looks to be the most accessible. Even though it feels a little fiddlier, working into the front loop is what twists the new stitch, tightening it and making it less visible.

Also, the way the stitch leans comes from the direction of the twist. In the case of the M1R you have just made, the front leg of the twist leans to the right.

MAKE °NE LEFT (M1L): LEFT-LEANING

This one is very similar to the MIR. The crucial difference is the direction in which you insert the needle under the running yarn.

SCAN T° WATCH
MY 'M1L' VID

STEP 1

Insert the tip of the left needle under the running yarn, this time going in from front to back, and lift it onto the left needle.

STEP 2

Knit into this new loop THROUGH THE BACK LOOP.

This also feels a bit awkward and fiddly, but again, it's what gives the stitch its lean. A closer inspection confirms that the leg that sits to the front of the twist is the one that slants upwards, and to the left.

MAKE °NE (PURL) INCREASES

It's perfectly possible to work purl versions of these decreases as well, either on the WS of the work or in sections of reverse-stocking-stitch on the RS. They are often called the 'Make One Right (Purl)' and the 'Make One Left (Purl)', abbreviated to 'MIR(P)' and 'M1L(P)' respectively.

I don't need to give you the steps, as they are pretty much the same as the ones we've just done. Just follow the above steps, working on the purl side, but where it says knit, purl!

TIP

It can be really hard to remember whether you are supposed to knit or purl through the front or back loop in any one of these four increases.

The way I remember it is related to the direction that I inserted the needle under the running yarn in Step 1.

If you go in from front to BACK, you work through the BACK loop, and if you go in from back to FRONT, you work through the FRONT loop. That's the same for both knit and purl versions.

As for remembering which increase requires which direction of entry in the first place, I'm afraid you're on your own with that… (Does it help to think: 'Make one leFFFFFt, FFFront to back'?)

KNIT FR°NT AND BACK (KFB)

Another type of single increase is the KFB. Instead of creating a new stitch out of a spare strand of yarn, this one works into the same stitch twice—as the name suggests, once into the front loop and once into the back loop—so that two new stitches are born from a single parent stitch. How modern!

The KFB is sometimes called a bar increase, because it makes a little horizontal bar of yarn that is quite visible on the front of the work. Many people call this a purl bump. Such foolishness! It LOOKS like one, so I understand the confusion, but how can it be? There is no purling in this increase! It's just a feature of how you twist from one stitch to the next, pulling one strand of yarn so that it runs horizontally across the front of the resulting stitch. Purl bump my Aunt Fanny!

The KFB is often rejected because of that bar—it's quite prominent—but the KFB has certainly earnt its stripes. For starters, it's really simple to work.

The brother of this increase is the 'Knit Back and Front', or 'KBF'. I won't patronise you by giving you the steps for this: just knit into the back loop of the stitch before the front loop, and there it is! Try them both out: see how they compare. You might find that you prefer one over the other. I can't imagine a situation where it would make much of a difference.

I find this type of increase a little clunky, and untidy: it doesn't sit very neatly in my knitting. You might quite like it, though, so don't take my word for it. *I* might be the odd one here. It wouldn't be the first time.

- -

TIP

If you are interested in a bit of further reading (homework!), look up the 'Lifted Increase', sometimes also called 'Make One Below'.

- -

SCAN T° WATCH
MY 'KFB' VID

STEP 1
Knit into the front loop of the next stitch on the left needle, but DON'T slip the old stitch off just yet.

STEP 2
With the parent stitch still on the left needle, take the tip of the right needle around to the back of the work, and knit into the same stitch *through the back loop*. This time you *do* slip the parent stitch off the needle, and the increase is complete.

DOUBLE INCREASES

Double increases, logically enough, create two extra stitches, resulting in three stitches from just one parent.

KNIT ONE, YARNOVER, KNIT ONE (KYOK)

I would say that this is my go-to double increase, and I'll use it wherever I can. It's perfectly symmetrical, which of course appeases the old CDO, and it's really easy to work. It has a nice flow and doesn't feel like it interrupts your knitting, which is more important than you might yet realise.

SCAN TO WATCH
MY 'KYOK' VID

STEP 3
Insert the tip of the right needle back into the parent stitch, through the front loop once again.

STEP 1
Knit into the parent stitch, but leave it on the left needle.

STEP 4
Complete the knit stitch, and *do* slip the parent stitch off the left needle, to complete the increase.

STEP 2
Make a yarnover around the right needle tip.
(Remember: it's anticlockwise.)

Examine this one closely. It looks like the centre stitch is a little bit recessed. That's because the first and third stitches are coming out of the front of the parent stitch just like any other knit stitch. That middle stitch, however, is the yarnover, and the working yarn was behind the parent stitch when the yarnover happened. You can't have all three stitches coming out of the front of the same stitch: there would be nothing to separate them and they'd end up as one utterly useless, ginormous, triple-sized single loop.

°THER INCREASES: AN °VERVIEW

There are SOOOOOO many other increases out there. I could devote an entire book to just this topic, and *still* probably never get through them all!

There is the PYOP, for example, which is just like the KYOK, but with purls instead of knits. And the KFBF, which is just like the KFB, but with an extra stitch in the front loop at the end. There is the KFPB (Knit Front and Purl Back!), not to mention the PFKB (Purl Front and Knit Back)!

Don't forget there is also a WS version of everything I've mentioned here. The list unfolds exponentially when you start taking all of those variables into consideration. It doesn't even stop there: what about increases that add *more* than two stitches to your stitch count? Imagine the KFBFBF, for example, or the KYOKYOK. And you can keep adding YOs and Ks to that as many times as you like, creating HUGE increases!

TIP

Call this homework if you like (or 'prep', if you are posh): why not work up a little swatch, experiment a bit using these principles, and have fun coming up with some increases of your own? You might think I'm joking, but you'll get a really good understanding of how things work—and I mean REALLY work—once you start trying to invent new stuff of your own.

Making stuff up is how I've learnt most of the things I know about knitting. Each time I wanted to put something in a pattern, but didn't know how to do it, I threw some yarn at some needles and tried it out. Nine times out of ten, I crashed and burned, but I always got there in the end.

Actually, the nine failed attempts taught me much more than the tenth, triumphant one. I often learnt WHY a certain thing wouldn't work, saving me a lot of time trying other things along the same lines. A wise man told me recently, 'You see more when you get lost.'

My aim here, friendly reader/knitter, is to make you fearless. It's all very well knowing how to follow a pattern, doing as you are told, and sticking to knitting things that you feel comfortable with, but how can you grow if you never push your own boundaries? Fear of failure is one of the most crippling things in the world. But once you throw away the fear of bollocksing everything up, and just give something a go, you'll find your knitting capabilities fly through the roof.

CABLES: AN °VERVIEW

I thought this was a knitting manual, not an electrician's guide… Rolls eyes.

Cabling in knitting has nothing to do with rewiring the kitchen. It is, rather, a method of allowing columns of stitches to cross over each other, creating complex and beautiful patterns in your knitting. If you can't picture what I'm talking about, think traditional Aran jumpers.

Cables have a sculptural, structural nature, which literally adds a whole new dimension to your work.

I remember when I first started all this stuff—I had made a few socks, so I was already quite comfortable with all of the techniques this book has covered so far. I looked at a cabled jumper and thought, 'I simply can't imagine how that is done. It must be horribly difficult.' And with that defeatist attitude, I convinced myself that I wouldn't ever be able to do anything as complicated as cables.

Later, when I realised how INCREDIBLY EASY they are, I kicked myself at the thought of all that lost time, when I was too afraid to take the plunge and give cabling a go.

This leads me on to what I consider to be a really important aspect of being a good knitter. I'll get back to the cables in a sec.

AN IMP°RTANT AND TIMELY PEP TALK

At the end of the last section, I talked about the value of fearlessness in your knitting. Let's examine that in a little more detail.

Fear. Knitting. Fear. *Knitting!* Do you see the point I'm making? It's *knitting*: what exactly is there to be fearful *of*?

Abso-bloody-lutely nothing, that's what!

What's the worst that can happen? You make a mistake. You go back and fix it. Big deal.

Worse? You might not be able to fix it and end up undoing it all. So what? No one died. The sun still comes up the next day, and shines on another opportunity to get it right.

There.   Is.   No.   Jeopardy.

I have a mantra that I use in my knitting, and I carry it through into the rest of my life as well:

No matter how complicated the finished project, it's only ever One Stitch at a Time.

One Stitch at a Time.

You might indeed look at a complicated cabled jumper, and think, I have no idea how to make that. But then you get told what the first stitch is, and you realise it's one you already know. Then you realise you know the next stitch as well, and you start looking at that jumper as a series of very small steps that you *already know how to do*. It's a simple matter of methodically working through each one in turn.

In life, it might be a massive project, involving hundreds of people, and hundreds of thousands of pounds. Daunting yes, but what's the first thing that needs to be done on the journey towards completing it? I suspect it will be something quite small and very manageable. Never confuse daunted with thwarted.

One Stitch at a Time.

I've shortened that to my own little hashtag: #OSAAT, and I use it all over the place. Have done for years.

Imagine my joy, then, when I was contacted by a very nice lady from Finland, called Jutta, who wanted to tell me that 'Osaat' is actually a Finnish word.

Gulp! It's bound to be something rude…

Far from it: in Finnish, the word 'Osaat', that I had already been using for years as a term of empowerment, actually means, 'you can', or 'you are able to'.

Seriously, dude.

It's serendipity at its most convoluted, and I may have actually shouted out loud when I read her email. And when I say, 'shouted out loud', you can assume I mean 'shrieked like an un-gendered thing that shrieks…'

So that's what I mean when I talk about fearlessness in your knitting. The realisation that there is nothing to be frightened of, that there is nothing you can do that can't be undone, or redone, and that no matter how big the task is, it can always be broken down into simple, manageable chunks.

Now look at that cabled jumper with fresh eyes. Instead of saying to yourself, 'I have no idea how to do that,' say, 'I wonder what the first stitch in that jumper is?'

WHAT IS A CABLE?

Essentially, a cable in knitting is a set of stitches that have been worked out of their normal order. Ordinarily, as you work along the stitches on your needle, you work them in the order in which they are presented to you. 1, 2, 3, 4, 5, 6, 7, 8 and so on.

If, however, you wanted to pop a '2 over 2' cable in there (I'll get to what that means in a mo), you might want to work stitches 5 and 6 *before* you work stitches 3 and 4. And this presents a problem: stitches 3 and 4 are in the way, and you can't *get* to stitches 5 and 6.

This is where your trusty friend the cable needle comes in. Your cable needle might be one of several shapes, but chances are, there will be a point at each end and a hump, curve, or bend, partway along it, just so that it doesn't fall out of your stitches when you let it go mid-manoeuvre. You use it to hold 'some' stitches out of the way, while you work 'some others'.

In our example above, we would put stitches 3 and 4 onto the cable needle, keeping them nice and safe, and then we can easily get at, and work, stitches 5 and 6.

Finally, we'd retrieve stitches 3 and 4 from the cable needle, and work them as well. Then we have successfully worked our stitches in the order: 1, 2, **5, 6, 3, 4**, 7, 8.

Ta-da!

Cables come in many shapes and sizes. They can look like twists of candy cane running vertically up your work, or they can travel diagonally across the fabric in sweeping lines. You can combine them in very elaborate ways, but generally speaking, the cabling itself is only a very small part of the overall design.

In a lot of cabled patterns, for example, you might only be working cables on every eighth row, or something like that. The rows in between will usually just be knits and purls. Bear in mind then, it's how you put the cables *together* that makes a pattern look complex, not the actual cable stitches themselves.

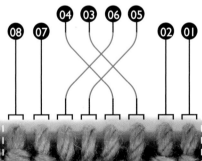

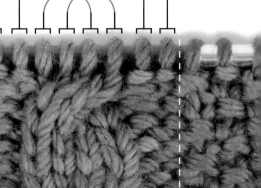

NAMING CABLES

Sometimes, you might be doing something simple like crossing one stitch over the stitch next to it. This would be a 'one-over-one' cable. Or possibly a '1x1' cable. And this is where explaining things can be a bit of a bear: there are lots of different ways of naming cables. Each designer will no doubt have their own preference (or perhaps be governed by a magazine's preferred naming style), so it's really important to look at the stitch key of your pattern to make sure you understand what type of cable is being specified in each case.

A column of stitches (or a group of columns of stitches) can either cross over the stitch or stitches to its left, or the ones to its right.

Most naming conventions will tell you how many stitches are involved, and in which direction they are supposed to cross. Or at least, all the *useful* ones will…

The convention that I usually use is a set of abbreviations that gives as much detail as possible about what you are supposed to be doing. For example, a cable that crosses two stitches over two, leaning to the right, would be called a 'C4B'.

Oh, right. Hang on, that doesn't look like it much describes anything. It does, but in a way I haven't explained yet.

The 'C' just stands for cable. So far, so good. This sends an alert to the knitter: cable coming up! The '4' tells you how many stitches in total are involved in this particular procedure. That just leaves us with the rather cryptic 'B'.

As I've said, cables will either cross to the right or to the left. Some naming conventions will specify 'R' or 'L', to let you know which way the cable needs to cross.

I use 'B' and 'F', which stand for 'Back' and 'Front' respectively, and there's a very good reason for that. Once you have transferred your stitches onto the cable needle, you need to get those stitches out of the way, so that you can get to the other stitches first. You have two options: you can either hold the cable needle in front of the work, or behind it. If you hold it to the front, your cable will cross to the left, and if you hold it to the back, the cable will cross to the right.

The reason I go for 'B' and 'F' instead of 'R' and 'L', is because some people struggle to remember whether crossing to the right requires the cable needle to go to the back or to the front. This way, the name of the cable itself tells you how to make it.

Putting all that together, 'C4B' gives you a cable that is made from four stitches, where one pair crosses to the right, over the other.

Admittedly, the name falls a bit short, as there is always the possibility that a four-stitch cable *might* consist of one stitch crossing over three, or three stitches crossing over one, but you can't have everything. I think that's one of the reasons why there has never been a standard naming convention: there are so very many—almost limitless—combinations, and so much information to try to get across. Different people have found different ways that make the most sense to them, trying to create order from chaos, and that's why you must always check the key in the pattern, and make sure that you understand the intentions of the designer.

Enough. Let's get on with doing one.

C4B (CABLE 4 BACK)

SCAN T° WATCH MY 'C4B/C4F' VID

STEP 1

Slip two stitches from the left needle onto the cable needle*.

STEP 2

Hold the cable needle behind the work. You can let go and it will just hang there.

STEP 3

Knit the next two stitches from the left needle.

STEP 4

Without turning or twisting the cable needle, knit the two stitches (individually) from the cable needle.

C4F (CABLE 4 FR°NT)

The steps for this one are exactly the same as the steps for the C4B, except that instead of holding the cable needle to the back of the work, you hold it at the front. Everything else is exactly as above. Knock yourself out.

THE°RETICAL CABLES

Don't worry, this isn't a mathematical treatise on the theory of working cables made from imaginary negative numbers, with infinite decimal expansions. Everyone breathes a massive sigh of relief.

The theory behind most simple cables can be stated as follows:

- STEP 1
  Put 'some' stitches onto the cable needle, holding it either at the front or the back.

- STEP 2
  Work 'some more' stitches from the left needle.

- STEP 3
  Work the stitches *from* the cable needle.

That's pretty much all there is to it.

Don't forget: whenever there is an instruction to slip some stitches, it will always mean purlwise, unless otherwise stated.

BUILDING A CABLE

A single cable stitch doesn't do a great deal on its own, except perhaps distort the fabric of your knitting a bit. It's only when you start to stack cables on top of each other, or create sequences of them with repeating patterns, that exciting and beautiful designs will start to emerge.

Many of the simplest cable designs feature columns of four or six stitches (or some other number), which twist round each other over and over again, as the column progresses. These are often referred to as rope cables, or twisted cables. (I don't think there's an official name, people just tend to use words that describe the stitch in a way that makes the most sense to them.)

With this kind of rope cable, it's likely that you would need several plain rows between each cable row: perhaps four, or even more, depending on how loose you want the twists to look.

Conversely, with what is called a 'travelling' cable, where a column of stitches moves diagonally across your knitting, you are more likely to work the cable every other row, to keep the diagonal line as smooth as possible. All of these things are subject to massive variation, however.

The C4B (or F) is perfect for a rope cable, but you can switch in any number you like, and create the cable of your choice, based on the same model. A 'C6F', for example, would have three stitches crossing over three, with the cable needle held at the front, and would therefore cross to the left. A C8B, then, would be four stitches crossing over four to the right, cable needle held at the back.

HAZARD

OK, you got me: yes, it's possible that a C6F could be four stitches crossing over two, or even two stitches crossing over four, but the standard assumption would be to divide the number evenly into two, particularly for a rope cable where the likelihood is that you want both parts of the cable to be the same size to keep the uniformity as the rope extends.

You're right to question me, of course, and that's why one should always read the pattern notes.

STUFF TO KNOW

I've thought long and hard about this, and I've come up with a naming convention that addresses the issue of 'the number'.

If you were to split the number in the name of the cable into two parts, the first part being the number of stitches that cross over the top of the others, and the second part, the number of stitches underneath, a C4F would then be rendered thus: C2:2F. That's one that doesn't really matter either way, but under the same rules, the ambiguous C5B becomes a C2:3B or even a C3:2B, and because of which number comes first, there is no ambiguity at all. C2:3B would have two stitches crossing over three, to the right, while C3:2B crosses three over two, also to the right. I don't know why I mentioned it really, as there's about as much chance of it becoming standard as I have of becoming a fish.

I want to examine the C4B and the C4F a bit more. You know how my brain works by now—I like to get into the (k)nitty gritty of *why* things turn out the way they do. 'How' on its own is just not enough! Besides, if you've stuck with the book this far, there's a pretty good chance that you like that sort of stuff too.

In both cases, there are two stitches that will travel across the work, and in both cases, those two travelling stitches cross over two other stitches.

Looking at the steps for both, let's isolate which stitches are the ones that travel. Are they the ones that go onto the cable needle (sounds plausible), or the ones worked immediately after slipping some stitches to the cable needle?

Actually, the correct answer is both. It depends on the direction of travel.

If crossing to the left, the stitches on the cable needle are the ones that do the travelling. If, however, the cable is travelling to the right, the stitches that move are not in fact the ones that go onto the cable needle, and are, instead, the ones that follow them.

It doesn't really matter whether you are aware of this fact or not, but one day you might want to improvise a cable pattern of your own, and it's useful to understand what is going on. If you were to assume that any stitches you put on the cable needle will be the ones that you see moving—as I suspect a lot of people assume, simply because they haven't really thought about it—then your cables will be a bit of a mess.

°THER TYPES °F CABLE

You can stick any number you like into that naming formula. A 'C7B' could be three stitches over four, or four stitches over three, crossing to the right (seeing as there is currently no all-purpose, highly useful naming convention doing the rounds…).

Depending on the type of fabric you are creating, you can do some pretty massive cables, like C18F, crossing nine stitches over nine, to the left. It's good to take into account, however, that this sort of cable yanks the moving stitches quite some distance away from where they started, so unless you are working with a very loose fabric indeed, things will start to get very bunched and distorted.

You can also combine cables with other types of stitches, such as decreases and increases. If you are making a cabled hat, for example, you might need your cables to get smaller as the crown of the hat diminishes. Or it might be that you simply need to reduce the stitch count to shape the top of the hat, and you have decided to hide those decreases in a cable. (Look out for that very situation in the pattern for the Slalom hat on page 157.)

The general rule here is that the decrease would be worked into the stitches that cross behind the travelling stitches, and thus, an otherwise obvious decrease stitch is completely obscured from view by the stitches that cross in front of it.

Tidy!

There are many hundreds of books out there devoted to cables, and I'm not really often given to hyperbole, but with the myriad types of cable stitch that can be invented, and the *millions* of combinations in which they can be combined, I have no hesitation in saying that the possibilities really are endless.

This should have given you enough knowledge of the theory of cabling, and of the building blocks of it, to be able to understand pretty much any type of cable you are likely to come across. Always remember to refer to the pattern key, however, to make sure you understand the required cables in the way the designer intended.

FINISHING
TECHNIQUES [CH.9]

Knowing how to knit loads of different types of stitches and doing lots of fancy things like cables is all very well: it will certainly give you many thousands of hours of pleasure over the years, and you will no doubt build up a huge collection of finished objects, from hats to socks and things to cover every body part in between (raises an eyebrow…).

The uninitiated out there will praise your focus and commitment, and wonder how on earth it's possible to do such amazing stuff with only two sticks and a bit of string.

It's not the whole story, though, by any means. And anyway, what do the uninitiated know?

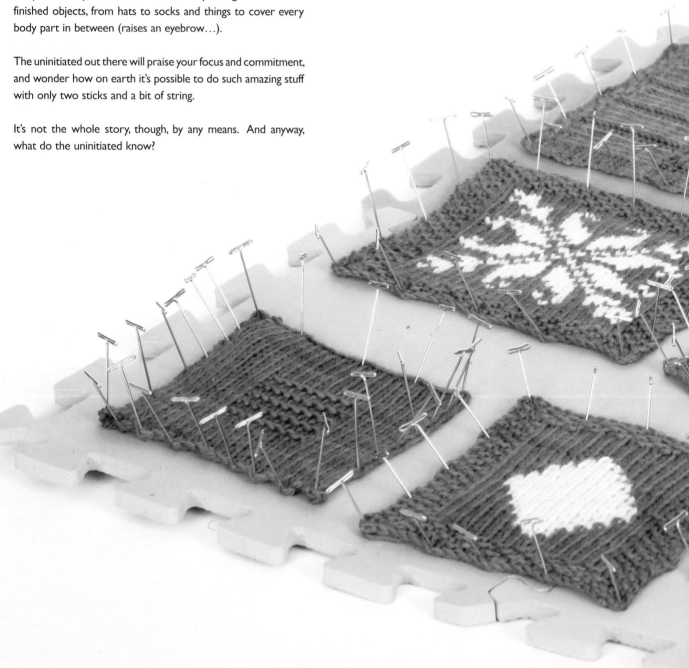

GLOSSARY

Knitters have lots of fun acronyms and initialisms to describe their projects in various stages of completion. Here are a few, so that you're not bemused in conversation with die-hard knitting fans:

NAP: Needle-Adjacent Project. This is a project that you haven't started yet, but you've sourced the pattern and the perfect yarn, and it will be the very next thing you cast on. (Pronounced like a short snooze.)

WIP: Work in Progress. Anything that is currently on your needles. You may only have completed the cast on, or you might be just about to cast off: it still counts. (Pronounced like 'whip'.)

PHD: Project Half Done. Interchangeable with the term 'WIP'.

FO: Finished Object. Officially, you can only truly call your project an FO once you have woven in all the ends, washed it and blocked it. (See page 120 for what that means.)

WHY BOTHER?

The thing that separates the dedicated, dyed-in-the-wool knitter (if you'll pardon the rather obvious pun) from the rank outsider or casual hobbyist, is the standard of finish.

Cue inspiring orchestral music, possibly 'Jerusalem'.

Turning a passably fun and lovable—possibly rather clumsy—piece of knitwear into a work of art that stands with its head held high, a masterpiece of precision, second in line to no one, is all about putting in place those little final touches that you may not think are really necessary, but once completed, transform your knitted item into something truly to be gazed upon in wonderment: inspiring awe and envy in all those who look upon it.

Sound of needle scratching record.

Okay, so maybe that's going a little overboard, but it's certainly true that there are lots of things that need to be attended to once the actual knitting side of things is over. Some might be aesthetic, some may have practical purpose, but all will elevate your work to a new level. The devil is in the detail after all.

WEAVING IN ENDS

Sometimes you might get lucky: you may have made a nice small item, like a hat, which only uses one colour and one ball of yarn. You're still going to have *two* ends of yarn hanging from your work: one at the very start, where you began casting on, and one where you've just finished.

If that's the case, you got off lightly. It's not unusual for larger-scale projects, particularly those that include lots of different colours, or that are made in lots of separate pieces, to leave the knitter with MANY ends to weave in once the knitting—the fun part—is over. (I'm guilty of perpetuating this: one of my scarf designs uses only four different colours of yarn, but because of *how* the colours are used throughout the piece, I had well over a hundred ends to weave in!)

For many people, this is a real chore. I have to say, I'm not a big fan myself—once I've finished knitting something, after maybe a couple of months of hard toil, I can't wait to start wearing it, or using it. The last thing I want to do is get my tapestry needle out and sit there for ages sewing!

It's a necessary evil, though, so whether you are one of these end-loving maniacs, or a normal person like me, it's worth learning a little bit about how to do it effectively.

Look, in all fairness, those ends aren't going anywhere—knitting doesn't unravel from the bottom up anyway, and how you finished casting off will prevent anything untoward from happening up there at the top, but those ends are just, well, tatty. You've put a lot of time and effort into that hat, surely you don't want to leave it looking half-finished, stumbling at the final hurdle?

There's a lot of information out there about the 'right' ways to weave in your ends. For garter stitch do this, for stocking stitch do that. And yes, there is something to be said for finding the perfect method that gives you exactly the result you want. I also believe it's easy to get bogged down in the mire of too much data. Worry too much about perfectly matching the stitch pattern/fibre blend/whimsical mood of the designer or whatever, and your task will prove exhausting and, no doubt, pretty fruitless.

As far as I'm concerned—and I know a lot of knitting purists will be screaming at me in frustration, but I simply don't care—the only things that really matter are that you tuck the end away somewhere where it won't be seen (at least, as much as is humanly possible!), and ideally, make sure that it won't work its way free at any point, letting your work look messy once again.

The well-trained knitter will have left about 15cm (6in) of yarn at the beginning and end of each section of yarn used, which is ample for weaving in. You will need a tapestry needle, or darning needle. (As long as the eye of the needle is large enough for the thickness of yarn that you are using, then you're good to go.) Thread the end of the yarn onto the needle.

Most of the things you make will have a right side and a wrong side. Logic dictates then, that you will be doing the weaving in on the wrong side, in order to try to minimise visibility.

First things first: if the end in question happens to be hanging out of the wrong side of the work already, all well and good. If, on the other hand, the end is popping out of the right side of the work, simply pass the needle through the fabric, taking it to the back.

NB: Make sure that you don't put the tip of the tapestry needle back into the same hole through which the end emerges, or things will become a bit unstable. It's best to go through the fabric via the hole nearest to where the end popped out.

Regardless of how scrupulously accurate—or slapdash—you might be, two major things are important in all cases:

- Whatever you are doing on the back of the work, you want to ensure it doesn't show through on the front. While you are working on the wrong side, it's best to keep checking the right side, just to make sure that nothing is amiss. This is particularly true when using multicoloured yarn.

- In order for the end to have the best chance of staying securely tucked away, you'll need to incorporate a few changes of direction.

It is, of course, perfectly possible simply to thread the yarn through a straight line of stitches and leave it at that. While that might hide the end away, it really won't be very secure. Don't forget, knitted fabric is very stretchy and has an enormous amount of give in it. The constant stretch and release of all the stitches holding your yarn in place will work it free in no time. That's incredibly annoying, particularly if you have finished weaving it in. No doubt you will have trimmed the end close to the fabric, meaning there won't be as much yarn left to play with if you end up having to go through the whole process a second time. Knitter beware…

Regardless of what stitch pattern you find yourself looking at on the wrong side of your work, I have found that the best thing to do is follow the path of a single strand of yarn as it makes its way through the knitting.

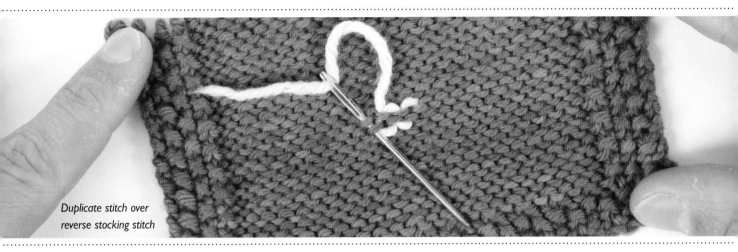

Duplicate stitch over reverse stocking stitch

If you stretch the existing stitches open, you'll be able to trace the journey of any given piece of yarn, tracking it as it goes under and over its neighbours, zigzagging up and down, and working its way along the row.

Using your tapestry needle, follow the line of your chosen strand either until you run out of usable yarn in the tail, or until you have traced the line of at least six to eight full stitches.

This method is often referred to as 'duplicate stitch', as you are literally duplicating the path the yarn takes through a stitch. It is also called a 'Swiss darn'—I have no idea why.

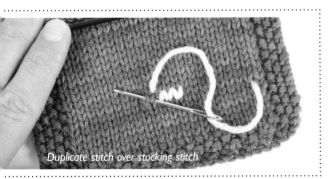

Duplicate stitch over stocking stitch

Too much bother? Well, I wouldn't blame you. I sometimes find that it's perfectly acceptable and effective just to catch the back half of a few stitches with the tapestry needle, actually splitting the strands of the yarn, taking the tail this way and that a few times, locking it in with each change of direction. Not as invisible, but that might not be important in some cases.

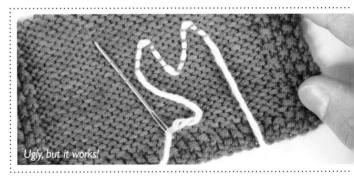

Ugly, but it works!

There are loads of ways to do this, and you'll no doubt find the ones that work best for you. I simply try to do as good a job as I can. It's never perfect. Neither am I. I'm totally cool with that.

When you are done, ordinarily you would just trim the end close enough to the fabric so that it doesn't stick out too far, but not so close that the end will disappear back into where it just came from. Yeah, I know: no hard and fast rule there either. Sometimes knitting just refuses to be caught in a bottle…

Many people advocate not trimming the end until after the knitting has been washed and blocked.

Oh, okay. Not until it has been washed and…wait, what?

BLOCKING YOUR WORK

One of the properties of natural animal fibres is that they have a memory. No, I don't mean that your favourite jumper carries with it memories of your granny, who made it for you when you graduated—although that's rather a nice thought—but it has a memory for *shape*. When wet, and when the fibres of the yarn have absorbed enough water to make them really pliable, you can 'train' your piece of knitting into the shape you want. Hold it in the new position until it dries, and hey presto! The memory of the old shape has been overwritten with this new and improved version.

That's it in a nutshell.

NB: Animal fibres do this trick the best. Plant-based fibres will block to a certain degree, but 100%-synthetic fibres won't really take a block at all.

One type of knitting that really *does* require a good block is lace. Often the patterns in a lace shawl are incredibly delicate, made more from holes than yarn, and of course, a hole has no structure: nothing to hold it in place. Just off the needles, most lace knitting looks like roadkill. It's only when you block it, sometimes stretching out the fabric to its fullest extent, that the beauty of the pattern will emerge. (Or it might be that the tank top you have just knitted for yourself isn't *quite* long enough, and a bit of a block *might just* claw back some extra centimetres, meaning you won't need to feel ashamed every time you breathe in, and out pops your belly button.)

You can get specific wool soaks—soft detergents formulated for natural fibres—which will help to soften the yarn, but if I can just lean in and whisper for a second, man to man: remember that we are the minority in a largely female-populated crafting world. I suspect the perfumes in most of these soaks aren't intended to appeal to the likes of you and me. I find them to be a bit cloying and overly feminine, but that's just a matter of personal taste. They certainly help with the task in hand, however. Some natural fibres can feel very coarse and scratchy and could do with softening up. A small amount of hair conditioner will also do the job. (Oft-heard euphemisms for scratchy yarn: toothy; precocious; got a bit of bite to it; characterful; rustic—people go to great lengths to avoid having to admit that some fibres are just downright rough!)

It has to be said, however, that a lot of the more…ahem…*unruly* yarns will soften quite an astonishing amount after they have been soaked and washed, which only really leads me to ask why that doesn't happen to them before you buy them. They'd be a lot nicer to work with, but I'm sure there is a perfectly valid reason, which someone will no doubt write in to tell me about.

Part fill a large bowl with some lukewarm water. The water should be not too cold and not too hot, otherwise the fibres will get a bit of a shock, making them more prone to felting.

Gently submerge your knitting into the water. The key word here with *every* instruction in this section of the book is 'gently'. I can't impress that upon you strongly enough.

The knitted fabric will catch lots of air in it, and will probably want to keep bobbing to the surface. GENTLY press it down into the water, pushing out as much air as you can, but DON'T wring it in your hands or anything brutal and foolish like that.

It can take upwards of half an hour for the fibres to really take on enough water to do the job well, but you can leave them for a good while longer just to make sure.

When you take your knitting out of the water, you will be tempted to wring out as much water from it as you can. This would be a disaster. *Never* wring it.

Under ANY circumstances.

The fibres are now at their most vulnerable. Having taken on all that water, they are now malleable and compliant, which is just what we want, but they are also at their most fragile.
Do not wring.

Squeeze or press the excess water out of the knitting, with no twisting or turning at all.

DO NOT WRING! All *right*, already…

The best thing to do is get a large towel and spread it out on the floor. Place the knitting, as flat as you can make it, onto the towel. Carefully roll the whole shebang up into a long sausage. I step on the towel sausage, which presses the rest of the excess water out of the knitting and into the (hopefully) more absorbing fibres of the towel. Whatever you do:

Do. Not. Wring.

Now you are ready to block your work!

You can block your knitting gently, or pretty damned aggressively, depending on how much you want to affect the fabric and what you need to achieve.

Either way, you'll need some kind of flat but spongy surface to lay your knitting on—foam mats, a mattress or even just your carpet with a towel laid out on it—and some pins to hold it in shape.

If only a very gentle block is required—and this can be a good way to even out any discrepancies in your stitch tension (but let's not kid ourselves: it ain't a magic wand…)—it might be enough simply to pat it into shape, making sure there aren't any kinks or creases, and ensure that all the lines that are meant to be straight are, in fact, straight.

For anything that requires more severe treatment, however, use pins to hold everything in place. You may be putting the yarn under quite a lot of tension during this process, so making sure that it is held safely and securely is always a good thing.

Remember that knitted fabric is really stretchy. It will stretch both horizontally *and* vertically. You'll see that the more you stretch it vertically, the narrower it becomes horizontally, and vice versa. It only contains a finite amount of yarn, after all. There is a balance, therefore, to be found between length and width.

HAZARD

The width of a pin is only very tiny. If the yarn is under a lot of tension, all of that tension will be concentrated on the very small width of that very small pin. Even a very basic knowledge of physics will suggest that this might not be such a good idea.

Use as many pins as you possibly can. Go overboard. Pin out every single stitch around the edge of your work, if you can get your hands on enough pins! (Just make sure that they are stainless steel—rust marks won't come out of your knitting. Ever!)

Once the knitting is pinned out to your satisfaction, leave it to dry thoroughly. Room temperature will do nicely: you don't need to crank the heating up to full blast, although it might be worth noting that if you live in a very cold house and it's the dead of winter, it might need a bit of help!

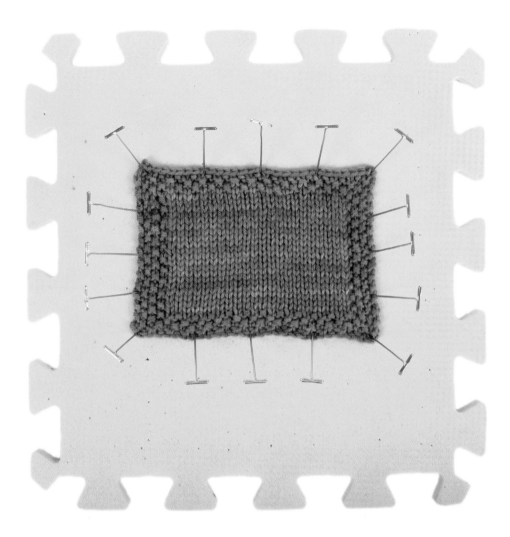

When your blocked knitting is completely dry, which might take a couple of days, you can take out all of the pins. Although you will no doubt see a little bit of spring back as you release the tension, it will pretty much stay in the new shape that you have created for it. It's like magic!

Another thing to be aware of here: stretching the yarn will change the nature of the fabric. Fresh off the needles, knitting is all bouncy and squishy. It feels really thick and luxurious. The harder you block that knitting, the more squish and bounce you take out if it. This is just a natural consequence of the process and not an indication that you have done anything wrong. The fabric will be much thinner, and it won't have the same propensity to spring back on itself that it had before. The upside of this is that it will have much more drape than it would otherwise have had, and for more delicate items, particularly lace shawls, this is definitely a silver lining.

There is certainly an argument that says the whole point of hand-knitted stuff is that it should be warm and cosy—a hand-made hug, if you will—so why would you want to do anything that would take that one key function of its existence away?

I hear you. I'm in that camp. I hardly block anything.

That's just the merest overview.

YouTube has a load of tutorials that can help you with the best ways to pin out different shapes for the best results. Go crazy. Or don't.

Some people even block their socks. I say that's what feet are for…

CHARTS [CH.10]

And jumping a massive 23 places, to become this week's number one designer…S°CKMATICIAN!!!

Not exactly.

You will by now be quite used to the way simple knitting patterns are written out. Line by line, row by row, the written pattern tells you in words—or rather, in abbreviations of words—what stitches to create and in what order. You're aware that repeated sections don't need to be written out over and over, that you can instead give the instructions for what to do in the repeat, and tell the reader that they need to repeat it a certain number of times. It's a brilliant method for conveying instructions from the designer to the knitter—it's been around for centuries and it works very well.

The one thing that a pattern written out in this way *doesn't* give you, however, is any information about how the stitches from one row stack up on top of the stitches from the one below, and the one below that. You might not think of that as a problem—after all, as long as you follow the instructions correctly, without errors, and do exactly what you are told, the stitches will naturally line up with each other as they are supposed to. And you would be totally correct in that assertion.

Well, my friend, I hate to break it to you: ain't no such thing as the perfect knitter. I like to think I'm pretty close (I know, revoltingly hubristic), but with the best will in the world, mistakes happen, and when they do, you'll want to be able to see what's going on.

Most of the time, of course, you'll be creating a nice, simple, logical pattern and it will be easy to see if things have gone a bit wonky. When you get used to it, you'll probably be able to deduce at a glance where that pear-shapedness began. You can't always rely on that being the case, though. With more complex textures, or with patterns that aren't as regular, it can be hard to see what is supposed to go where.

It's not all about mistakes, either. Before you've had the chance to get familiar with how a pattern is supposed to look as it develops, it might be that you want to see how all the stitches are supposed to line up on top of each other, just to make sure you're on the right track, and to be certain that you *haven't* made any errors in your work. There's nothing worse than not knowing if what you have done is correct or not. How can you possibly continue with confidence if there's a chance it might already have gone wrong! This is the major area where written instructions fall down.

Wouldn't it be amazing, then, if there were a way to show on a page, what your knitting should look like in real life?

Charts. Brassy fanfare!

Essentially, a chart is just a diagram of what you are knitting. It's a grid of squares—oh, all right then: they are actually more often rectangles, to better represent the aspect ratio of a knitted stitch, you pedantic swine, you!—where each stitch to be worked is represented by a 'square' on the chart. One row on the chart represents one row of your knitting, and the number of rows on the chart equals the number of rows that you are supposed to knit.

Symbols on the chart represent specific stitches in the pattern, and there will be a key accompanying the chart, telling you what each symbol means. Unfortunately, there is no standard set of symbols, as there are so many different types of stitch (just think of the different types of cables alone…), and different patterns require different things. It would be lovely to think that this stuff could be formalised into one coherent language, but I wouldn't hold my breath on that front. Some conventions have arisen, however, and you will see the same symbol being used across various designers' charts. ALWAYS check the chart key to make sure that what you are seeing and what you are doing match up.

Swatch from Chart A

Key:

☐	RS: Knit, WS: Purl.
⊡	RS: Purl, WS: Knit.

CHART A

Row numbers (left side, bottom to top): 2, 4, 6, 8, 10, 12, 14, 16, 18, 20, 22, 24, 26, 28

Row numbers (right side, bottom to top): 1, 3, 5, 7, 9, 11, 13, 15, 17, 19, 21, 23, 25, 27

Stitch numbers (bottom, right to left): 24 23 22 21 20 19 18 17 16 15 14 13 12 11 10 9 8 7 6 5 4 3 2 1

Have a look at Chart A, in the top-right corner of this page, and its accompanying key.

In a nutshell, charts are worked from bottom to top, with RS rows worked from right to left, and WS rows worked from left to right. That actually makes good sense, if you think about which direction you knit in.

Always follow the numbers. Row numbers are positioned at the start of a row; their position tells you which side of the chart to start reading from on any given row. Stitch numbers along the bottom will go from right to left, as that is the direction you would normally knit the first row of a chart.

When knitting flat, one works the first row, knitting from right to left. Then, when you turn your knitting, you work along the second row, going back in the opposite direction. The same is true on the chart: the first row (and subsequent odd-numbered rows) is read from left to right, and the second row (and subsequent even-numbered rows) is read from left to right.

Now let's look at what the symbols in the squares mean.

The first eight rows of the chart alternate between a row of empty squares, and a row of squares with dots in them. I can tell you that this is going to give us eight rows of garter stitch. And that makes sense, because as we know, garter stitch looks like a row of knits, followed by a row of purls, and so on. The slightly tricky concept to grasp here, is that the chart shows how the finished knitted item will *look*, rather than showing us how it was made.

Huh?

Well, as I've just said, we know that garter stitch *looks* like rows of knits alternating with rows of purls, but we also know that when it is worked flat, every row is *knitted*. If we knitted the RS rows, and purled the WS ones, as the chart seems to be suggesting, we would end up with stocking stitch.

This is where the key is really important.

See the bit on the key that refers to the empty square? The legend reads: 'RS rows: Knit, WS rows: Purl'.

This means that every time you see an empty square on an RS row (in this case, all the odd-numbered rows), you will knit it. And if you see an empty square on a purl side row, you would purl it. Same symbol, different instruction for each side.

The reverse is also true. The next legend on the key, next to the dotted square tells you: 'RS rows: Purl, WS rows: Knit'.

Putting these two things together, and looking back at the chart, it tells us this:

On the first (RS) row, the empty squares tell us to knit. On the second (WS) row, the dotted squares tell us to also knit.

This part of Chart A, then, tells us to knit the first eight rows.

That seems to be much more complicated than it probably needs to be, but we can see the results in the picture called 'Swatch from Chart A', in the top-left corner of the last page.

On the right side, you will see that it looks like a row of knits, a row of purls, a row of knits, and a row of purls, and so on, even though every row was knitted. And that's *exactly* what those eight rows on the chart look like! *That's* why things are charted out like that: it's so that the finished product looks exactly like what you see on the chart, and that makes it a lot easier to relate one to the other.

Now let's move on to the next eight rows.

Looking back at Chart A (above left), you can see that we are making an eight-stitch border of garter stitch at the start of each row (again, you can tell it's garter stitch from the alternating rows of knit symbols and purl symbols), a central patch of stocking stitch (again, we know it is going to be stocking stitch, because all of the symbols *look* like knit symbols, and stocking stitch shows as all knit stitches on the RS), and the rows end with another garter-stitch border, matching the one at the beginning.

It's the stocking-stitch panel in the middle of the rows that I want to focus on here.

On the odd-numbered rows—all the RS rows—the chart key tells us that an empty square is knitted on the right side. So far, so good. The even-numbered rows—the WS rows—also have empty squares, and the chart key tells us that on a WS row, these squares should be purled. If you remember, a purl

stitch is just a knit stitch worked from the other side, so on the right side of the work, regardless of how they were created the stitches from both odd- and even-numbered rows all show as knit stitches, giving us stocking stitch, and again, that's exactly what the chart looks like.

It's a funny old concept to grasp at first, but once you get your head around it, it does actually make sense. You just have to keep your wits about you a little bit, and remember whether you are on a right- or wrong-side row, so you know which stitch you are meant to be working at any point.

If the chart simply told you what to do line by line, without this RS/WS delineation, what you would see on the chart would end up not looking anything *like* the pattern that you see emerging under your needles and would end up getting very confusing indeed.

Swatch 2 (below left) is what you would end up with if you knitted from exactly the same chart (Chart A), but worked every stitch on every row taking the symbols at face value, instead of having a WS alternative.

As you can see, the reults are very different indeed.

And if you wanted the results in Swatch from Chart A, but wanted a chart where you could just knit the symbols as you see them, as you can see from Chart B (below), it actually looks like Swatch 2 instead of Swatch from Chart A. Ultra confusing, and proves that the current way of doing things is in fact the best.

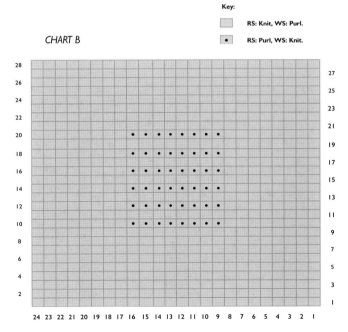

Key:

RS: Knit, WS: Purl.

• RS: Purl, WS: Knit.

CHART B

Many, if not most, patterns will include written instructions as well as charts, so if you are a chart-reader, like me, you can follow the chart, but if you absolutely hate reading charts, as some knitters do, you can work from the written instructions. Either way, it's actually quite useful to have both: if you get into a pickle at any point, it can be handy to have the other set of instructions right there: you can get a second opinion, as it were, about what you are supposed to be doing at that point.

If I may be permitted to offer a gentle and well-intentioned piece of advice here, though, it would be:
BLOODY WELL LEARN TO READ CHARTS!

Seriously, mate, I can't tell you how much time it will save you in the long run. Having a chart means glancing at a picture and relating it to what you have already done. All the information you need about which stitch you are supposed to work next, and which stitch from the row below it should sit on is right there in front of you. This really helps keep you on track.

It's also great if you haven't touched your knitting for a while. One glimpse of the chart can get you back on track, without having to wade through pages and pages of text, just to figure out where in the pattern you stopped.

Sometimes, there's no need for a chart. If the pattern is more about construction than stitch texture, there might not be any point in charting it out stitch by stitch. That's perfectly fine, but I can honestly think of NO GOOD REASON why there are so many knitters out there who resist learning to read charts. Believe me, they exist, and they don't know what they are missing. I really hope you won't put yourself among them.

READING CHARTS FºR KNITTING IN THE RºUND

This is actually simpler than working from a chart for knitting flat. When you knit in the round, there is no turning of the work, so you never work a WS row. Consequently, all that RS/WS stuff I've just covered doesn't apply here. If you see an empty square, you are going to knit it, regardless of whether you are on an odd- or an even-numbered row.

Hurrah!

TIP

Here's a little tip to tell you whether the chart you are looking at is supposed to be worked flat, or in the round. Where are the row numbers? For a chart that is worked flat, they alternate from side to side going up the chart. In the round, they will all be on the right-hand side. Again, that's because every side is an RS row.

NB: It's worth pointing out here that whether flat or in the round, you always read the chart starting at the bottom and working your way up.

Two of the five patterns in this book use charts. I have included the written instructions as well, for reference, but I urge you, as much as it is possible for the writer of a book to urge the reader, to train yourself to work from the charts first and foremost, and only to go to the written word for corroboration or clarification if you get stuck. I promise you, you'll thank me down the line.

°THER TYPES °F KNITTING [CH.11]

Ha! As if I could distil the rest of the world of knitting into one chapter! Not possible. I don't think I'll live long enough to learn everything there is to know about this fascinating craft.

Think of this chapter then, as just a few bullet points, or flash cards, to let you know some terms that you might want to look at in more detail in the future.

STRANDED KNITTING

Remember all those Fair Isle jumpers and tank tops from the 70s? That's stranded knitting.

Some people use the two terms interchangeably, but while all Fair Isle is stranded knitting, not all stranded knitting is Fair Isle.

In its most basic form, stranded knitting uses two colours of yarn per row, and complex and intricate patterns can be built up by knitting some stitches with one yarn and some with the other. The yarn that is not in use for any given stitch creates a strand—called a float—across the back of the work, making the fabric very sturdy, thick and warm. Perfect for winter on a remote Scottish island, in fact.

The floats not only add thickness to the fabric, but being straight, they hardly have any elasticity, and don't allow the fabric to stretch the way ordinary knitting does. For this reason, you must be careful with the tension of your floats. Too tight, and the front of the work will pucker. Too loose, and the fabric will lose its structure.

This type of knitting is most often worked in the round. It's not so easy to see what is happening when you're working on the wrong side, and working in the round means never having to turn the work. (That's not to say you CAN'T do stranded knitting flat. You can, and I often do —see above for proof!)

There are some pretty hefty limitations to the types of design that can be worked in this way: too many stitches of one colour at a stretch, and the float across the back gets too long. That not only causes problems with tension, but your float can also get snagged on fingers or clothing. Some people say that more than five stitches of the same colour is too many, some say seven, but everyone agrees that you have to keep the numbers down.

Stranded knitting is wonderful for adding a touch of interest to the yoke of a jumper (that's the bit across the chest, shoulders and the top of the back), and these days you are much more likely to see that sort of thing than a garment that uses stranded work throughout. Tastes change, and even though a lot of knitters today like the idea of a little bit of colourwork, the thought of making a whole garment that way is a bit daunting.

INTARSIA

Intarsia (the knitting technique, rather than the woodworking method of the same name) is a way of adding blocks of colour to your hand knits. The blocks can be any shape or size. They can be used to build up eye-boggling geometric patterns or even intricate pictures with many different colours, rather like a paint-by-numbers sort of affair. Whether the pattern is simple or complex, every separate block of colour requires its own length of yarn, usually wound around a bobbin for ease of use.

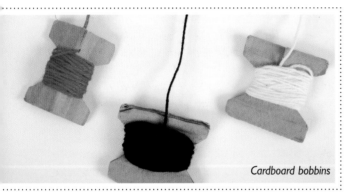

Cardboard bobbins

Unlike stranded knitting, there are no floats carried across the back of the work. Instead, the two yarns are twisted around each other wherever two coloured blocks meet, locking the two sections of the knitting together, as if two old friends were walking down the street with their elbows linked.

As you work across a row, once you have knitted the last stitch of one colour, it is important to introduce the new colour by bringing the new yarn into play from underneath and to the right of the old. This twists the two yarns together at that point, and nicely secures everything in place. The old yarn is then left hanging there at the back of the work, until you need it again on the next row.

Once you have turned the work, you'll be purling back on the wrong side. The concept here is no different. Every time you

need to work with a new colour, pick up the new yarn from underneath and to the right of the old one. The only difference is that on the WS rows you are purling, so the new yarns will present themselves to you from the front of the work. Similarly, on these rows, you leave the old yarns hanging at the front of the work, rather than at the back, until you need them again.

One of the major drawbacks to using this technique is tangling. Having lots of little bobbins of yarn hanging off your work can make the process of untangling them very arduous indeed. Try as you might, it's bound to happen. I think this is the main reason the technique seems to have fallen out of favour.

To be honest, although most intarsia knitting is done in stocking stitch, as that is the smoothest canvas upon which to showcase the design, there's no reason at all why you couldn't use different textures to add other dimensions to the pattern.

Back in the 1980s, designer Kaffe Fassett rose to prominence with his wildly colourful intarsia designs for jumpers, blankets and home furnishings.

These days, though, tastes tend more towards simpler, cleaner and more elegant designs, and the overly busy, multicoloured patterns of yesteryear have largely become a subject of mirth, or even ridicule, even though they took immense skill and great patience to create and make.

I wouldn't be at all surprised if intarsia weren't set to make a bit of a comeback, though. People are getting a bit more adventurous in their knitting again and starting to look to take their skills in new (to them) directions.

DOUBLE-KNITTING

Now we're talking! (And what we're talking about is the technique, not the yarn weight…)

Double-knitting, or DK, is *definitely* where I feel most at home. I'm fanatical about it, and evangelical about sharing this fascinating and beautiful technique with as many people as I can. I teach classes on the subject all over the world. In fact, I often get referred to as the <u>Dar</u><u>K</u> Lord of DK!

Standard, two-colour double-knitting is a way of creating a two-sided, reversible piece of fabric (in two colours, obvs!), with the pattern and colours on one side reversed on the other. For example, a black design on a white background on the front will show as a white design on a black background on the back.

Many people are intimidated by DK, as the results can be utterly breathtaking, but it is a LOT easier than you might think.

Stitches are set up on the needle, alternating with a knit stitch in one colour (for the front face of the fabric) and a purl stitch in the other colour (which will show on the other side as a knit stitch). This gives you the texture of stocking stitch on both sides.

The unit of double-knitting is a *pair* of stitches, rather than a single stitch, and the golden rule of DK is this:

Whatever you do to the first stitch of the pair, you do the exact opposite to the other.

This means that in any one *pair* of stitches, there will always be one knit stitch and one purl stitch, and there will always be one stitch of one colour and one stitch of the other.

Holding both colours at the same time, you work across the row, knitting the first stitch of the pair with Yarn A, bringing both yarns to the front, purling the second stitch of the pair with Yarn B, then returning both yarns to the back of the work, ready to start again.

When following a chart, each square represents one pair of stitches. The colour of each square tells you which colour to *knit* the first stitch of the pair with. The golden rule tells you that you must then *purl* the second stitch of the pair with the opposite colour. There's not much more to it than that!

Wherever you change colours mid-row (instead of knitting with Yarn A and purling with Yarn B, you then knit with Yarn B and purl with Yarn A), the yarn that has been on the front face of the fabric goes to the back, and the yarn that has been on the back face of the fabric comes to the front. This crossing over from front to back and from back to front locks the two faces of the fabric together.

There is nothing that you can do in single-face knitting that can't also be done in double-knitting. That includes textured stitches, lace, cables, shaping, etc. The joy is that you can include the option of two colours in all of these techniques and create different effects that just wouldn't be possible in any other field of knitting.

Double-knitting is twice as thick, twice as soft and twice as warm as single-face knitting. There is no unsightly wrong side to the work—both sides are equally beautiful, making it the perfect choice for scarves, shawls and anything that doesn't have a private side. There are also no limitations on how many stitches of one colour you can have at a stretch, as there are no floats to worry about: where one colour is creating stitches on the front, the other colour is creating stitches on the back, and this evens everything up nicely.

It is also true that it has double the number of stitches and takes double the amount of time. I don't deny that. I counter that argument though, by saying we knit because we enjoy it.

Double-knitting, therefore, is double the fun!

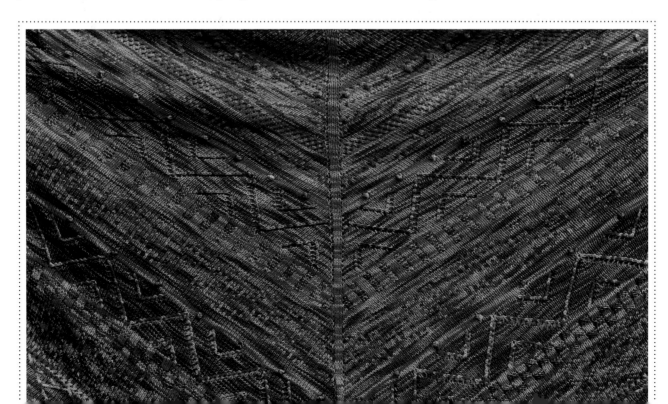

BRIOCHE KNITTING

Two-colour brioche is a sculpturally textured style of knitting, with a very three-dimensional look to it. In its most basic form it looks like a kind of rib stitch, with columns of knit stitches of one colour interspersed with columns of purl stitches of another. The difference between brioche rib and standard rib, apart from there being two colours, is that every stitch is given a yarnover of the opposite colour as it is created, then on the subsequent row, the stitch and its yarnover are worked together. This gives the texture of the fabric much more bounce and squish than a normal rib as there is more yarn being worked into every stitch than would usually be the case. It also explains brioche's unique appearance.

Traditionally, brioche is worked in two passes. On the first pass, you knit each knit stitch together with its yarnover (this is called a <u>br</u>ioche <u>k</u>nit stitch, or a 'bark'). You then slip each purl stitch, while at the same time giving it a yarnover of the opposite colour.

At the end of the row, you slide the stitches back to the other end of the needle, without turning the work, ready to do the second pass with the second colour. This time, you slip all the *knit* stitches, while giving them a yarnover of the opposite colour (remember these are the stitches that were worked in the first pass, so don't need to get worked now), and work each *purl* stitch together with its yarnover. This is called a <u>br</u>ioche purl, or rather amusingly, a 'burp'.

At the end of two passes, you will have worked every stitch once, and given every stitch a yarnover ready to be worked on the next row.

The visual aspect of brioche is very arresting and looks incredibly complex. Using decreases and increases, you can send the columns of stitches off in all sorts of interesting and beautiful directions.

Most of the brioche knowledge we have in the world today has been developed by knitting genius Nancy Marchant. The technique has really come into the spotlight in recent years, however, through the work of superstar designer Stephen West, who can really be credited with bringing brioche to the masses through his accessible and imaginative designs.

TROUBLESHOOTING: WHAT TO DO WHEN THINGS GO WRONG [CH.12]

It's all very well learning all this new stuff and adding new skills to your collection, but what happens when you make a mistake?

One of the things that puts new knitters off more than anything else, is the panic that sets in when they realise they have ballsed something up and have no idea how to put it right. All too often, this results in the knitting getting put aside, never to be picked up again.

I've alluded to this before, but I firmly believe that the way to a happy knitting future lies in being utterly fearless with your work. That's not just in the fearlessness of trying new things, but also in the fearlessness of making mistakes, and in the knowledge that if you do make a mistake you'll know how to fix it.

One of the things that will help with this is knowing that there is nothing that you can do in knitting that can't be undone. As I've already said: zero jeopardy.

That's not to say that there won't be times when you'll make a total mess of things. I do it all the time. Sometimes, when trying to fix a problem, I end up getting myself in even more of a tangle, and have to resort to some pretty drastic measures, but there's always a way out.

I'm going to go through some of the troubleshooting techniques that are out there, in what I consider to be the order in which you should attempt them. If the first one doesn't work, move on to the next, and so on.

TINKING

Funny word: to tink. It's a verb, and although you probably won't have heard it before, I've just surprised myself by finding out that it now exists as an official word on the Oxford English Dictionary website! Until this very moment, I thought it was just something that only knitters said, as an example of jargonish knitters' slang, but it seems to have gained enough usage in the wider world to qualify as an actual, recognised word!

Etymologically, 'TINK' is the word 'KNIT' spelt backwards. The act of tinking is the act of undoing your knitting, one stitch at a time, safely and easily, in order to go back the place where you made an error, so that you can fix it. (Annoyingly, because I'm me, I've always thought a more accurate term would be 'UNKNIT', as knitting backwards is something else entirely…)

It's great for when you spot a mistake that was only made a few stitches back, ideally on the same row that you are currently working on. Tinking back multiple rows can be time-consuming, and demoralising, but it's a very useful remedy for a more recent error.

The following steps demonstrate how to tink back in stocking stitch. The principles are the same for any other type of stitch, but when you are working with decreases and increases, things might look a little different. I don't have the space to go into all the different options for all the different types of stitch, but once you have grasped the basics, you'll be able to apply them to any situation you might find yourself in.

SCAN T° WATCH
MY 'TINKING' VID

STEP 1
Insert the tip of the left needle into the *parent stitch* of the first stitch on the right needle (this is the loop that the first stitch on your right needle comes out of). You should enter the parent stitch through the centre of the stitch, going in from front to back.

NB: If the stitch you are entering happens to be a twisted stitch, you will need to enter it from back to front.

STEP 2
Slip the stitch off the tip of the right needle, letting it hang free (it won't go anywhere, as you have the stitch below it caught on the tip of the left needle).

STEP 3
Give a little tug on the working yarn, and the loop of yarn coming through the parent stitch will pop free. The stitch itself will be nice and safe from unravelling because it has been neatly placed back on the left needle. Repeat Steps 1–3 as many times as necessary until you have returned to the scene of the crime, and are at the point when you have gone back *just past* the error, and you can now re-knit the offending stitch (or stitches) correctly, pretending it had never happened!

DR°PPING D°WN

If your error is a little bit further back—perhaps a couple of rows below your needles—and you don't fancy the idea of tinking back that far, it is possible to access the errant stitch from the top of the column that houses it.

Let's say you have spotted a purl stitch that should be a knit stitch, three rows down. Yes, you could tink three entire rows, but for the sake of just one stitch, dropping down can often be a much better option.

Grab a small crochet hook. This will be your best weapon in the fight against this sort of problem.

SCAN T° WATCH
MY 'DR°PPING D°WN' VID

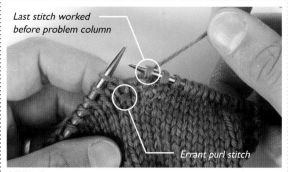
Last stitch worked before problem column
Errant purl stitch

STEP 1
It's usually better to keep going forwards, rather than going back to the point where you found the error. Keep following your pattern as instructed, until you have worked the stitch at the top of the column BEFORE the one where the naughty stitch is misbehaving.

STEP 2
Slip the stitch at the top of that column off the left needle. It's okay. I know there is a risk that it will unravel all the way down, but if you pinch the knitting just below the mistake, you'll stop it from going any further.

Running yarn, before and after the stitch

STEP 3
Insert your crochet hook under the running yarn that goes from your free stitch to the stitch that comes either immediately before, or immediately after it. It doesn't matter which you choose—go with whichever one is the more easily accessible to you.

STEP 4
Carefully, so as not to pull any yarn out of the stitches either side, ease the loop of your free stitch out of the stitch below it. You now have a *new* free stitch, one row lower than the one you started with, and a new loose strand of yarn running directly from the column *before* your free stitch to the column *after* your free stitch.
This strand is the first 'rung' of a ladder that you are about to create in your work (and is the reason this technique is also often referred to as 'laddering down').

STEP 5
Repeat Steps 3 and 4 as many times as necessary, until you have reached the stitch that needs fixing. Go ahead and pull that one out as well.

STEP 6

Insert the head of the crochet hook into the current free stitch, going in from front to back, ensuring that you haven't twisted the stitch in any way.

STEP 7

Catch the bottom rung of your ladder (the rung directly above the free stitch) with the crochet hook, going in from *under* the rung, and draw that rung strand through the *stitch* on your hook.

STEP 8

Assuming that the stitches you need to rebuild as you go up the ladder are all knit stitches, repeat Steps 6 and 7, until you have turned the last rung into a stitch, then just place it back on the left needle, ready to continue with your knitting.

Just be sure to replace it on the left needle mounted the correct way. This will mean inserting the tip of the left needle through the stitch that is on the crochet hook, going in as if you were going to slip it knitwise from the right needle to the left, in ordinary knitting (that means going in from right to left, and from front to back).

NB: If you find that instead of all knit stitches on your way back up the ladder, you also have some purl stitches to rebuild, the easiest thing to do is turn the work over, so that the purl stitch presents itself to you as a knit stitch. Then you can simply repeat Steps 6 and 7, but from the back of the work. After that, you turn the work again, and continue on up the ladder as before.

HAZARD

Dropping down is not necessarily recommended if you have a complicated stitch pattern to work with, as it can be really tricky to see which rung of the ladder is supposed to be which type of stitch.

It's also important to do it all with the utmost care not to distort the stitches either side of the ladder, or the fix will be quite visible and obvious once you have finished. No one wants baggy-arsed stitches in their work.

RIPPING OUT

Sometimes, it's just not possible to fix your error in either of the ways mentioned above. Perhaps the error is SO large and complicated that trying to fix it would take longer than actually re-knitting the project from scratch, or perhaps you have got yourself so confused, that you simply have no idea what to do to get back on track. In that case, sometimes the only thing for it is to rip out your work.

Ripping out your knitting simply means taking the needles out of all of the stitches, and pulling on the working yarn, unravelling everything, either until you have gone back further than where the big mess-up was, or until there is nothing left at all, except what looks like a massive pile of yarn noodles.

Ripping out all the way is often called frogging. Why frogging? Well, when you frog your work, you 'rip it, rip it, rip it!' (Say it out loud if you still don't get it. Don't shoot the messenger—I didn't make this crap up…)

Let's say, though, that you have ripped your work back to a point before you buggered it all up, but there is still enough decent knitting in your hands to be worthwhile trying to save it.

You now need to get all of those live stitches back on the needle, before they start unravelling further, and end up making even more of a mess than you had before. You don't want to end up frogging everything.

Choose which end to start with and begin inserting the tip of your needle into each stitch in turn.

It's a good idea to do this with a needle that is smaller than your working needle, otherwise you will probably pull some of the stitches out of their parent stitches as you go along, and that can make things a bit tricky. And horribly annoying.

We've talked about how a stitch is mounted on the needles before, and yes, it's important that they *eventually* end up mounted the correct way for knitting into. At this point however, I think it's WAY more important to secure them first, any way you can. Even if you split the yarn and end up with only part of the stitch on the needle, at least it won't go anywhere.

Some people will scream and clutch their pearls at hearing me say that, but I stand by it: get those stitches on the needle as soon as possible, however they land! Once they are all safe, you can breathe again. Then you can set about remounting them, and fixing any other problems, at your leisure, and without panic.

Once I have got all the stitches back on the needle, I sometimes go for a walk to get some fresh air. I then work across the row, slipping all of the stitches from the left needle to the right. If the stitch is already correctly mounted, with the trailing leg in front, I slip it purlwise.

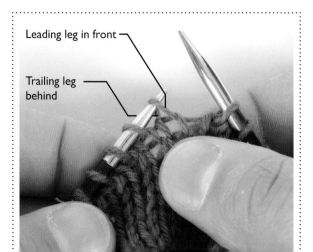

Leading leg in front

Trailing leg behind

If the stitch is mounted any other way, which depends on how it was picked up, you might find you need to do a bit of slipping it this way and that, until it is mounted how you want it.

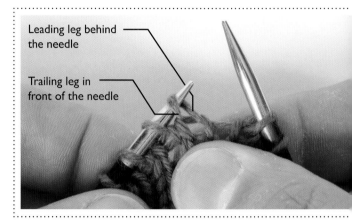

Leading leg behind the needle

Trailing leg in front of the needle

In cases like the one above, slip the next stitch knitwise, from left needle to right, then slip it purlwise back to the left. That will mount the stitch the way you want it.

TIP

If you care to know, there *is* a formula for picking up live stitches, in such a way that they are mounted correctly already:

If you are holding the needle tip in your right hand, and picking up the stitches by working along the row from right to left, you need to insert the right needle tip into each stitch from the back to the front.

If, on the other hand, you are going the other way, working across the row from *left* to *right*, with the needle tip in your *left* hand, then you need to insert the needle tip into each stitch rom the *front to the back*

That's an ideal-world scenario, of course.

We don't live in one of those...

LIFELINES

If you are about to embark on a very complicated section of your pattern, and you sense a fair chance of royally cocking things up, you might want to insert a lifeline into your work *before* jumping in. (I hate even *saying* this, as I'm all about a gung-ho attitude, and fearlessness, but sometimes a bit of realism doesn't go amiss.)

A lifeline is simply a length of yarn that is usually thinner, *smoother,* and in a contrasting colour to your main yarn (and therefore easily visible), that you can work into one of the rows of your knitting, prior to starting a tricky section. Dental floss works well. I'm not joking.

If you are using interchangeable knitting needles, there is a pretty good chance that there will be a little hole through the back end of the tip, for tightening the tip onto the cable.

If this is the case, take your lifeline, thread it through the hole, and tie a small, unobtrusive knot to secure it.

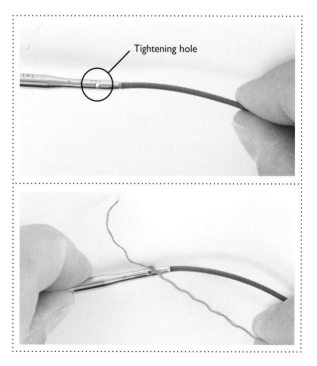

Tightening hole

Then, as you work your way along the next row of your knitting, the lifeline yarn will be pulled through the stitches without you needing to do anything.

If you don't have that handy little hole, thread your lifeline yarn onto a tapestry needle, and pass it through each loop on your left needle. Working from right to left, go into each stitch as if to purl, before you knit the next row.

Either way, your lifeline is now in place, going across the entire width of your knitting, and you can set off on the tough stuff with confidence.

Should the worst occur, and everything does in fact go tits up, you can simply take your needles out of your knitting, and rip back until you reach the lifeline. You won't be able to rip back any further than that, and the lifeline holds every stitch in place.

All safe and secure

Then you can simply transfer each stitch back onto the needle, slipping them all from the lifeline purlwise, knowing that a) they can't go anywhere and that b) they are already mounted the right way. Peace of mind. Easy.

TIP

You can also insert a lifeline *after* the event, so even if the big screw-up wasn't expected, you can still get the lifeline in place, before starting the big rip.

Simply locate a row somewhere safely below where the horror happened, and with the lifeline yarn threaded onto a tapestry needle, pick up the right-hand leg of each stitch in the 'safe' row.

Picking up the right leg rather than the left leg will ensure that your stitches are automatically mounted the right way, and you can rip back to the lifeline with Gay Abandon. Whoever she is.

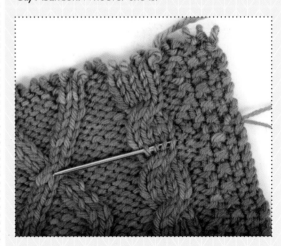

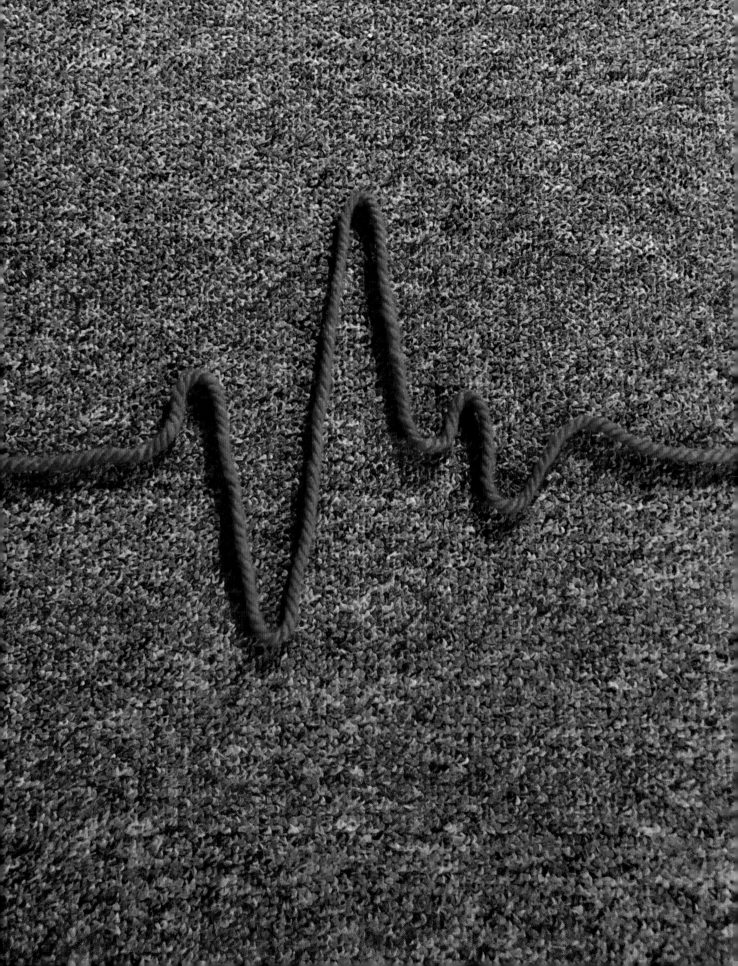

PATTERNS [CH.13]

It's now time to put all of your new-found skills into action. A vast amount of theory is all very well, but the proof of the pudding is in the eating, the proof of the theory is in the practice, and the proof of the knitting is in the patterns!

I have very carefully created and curated a collection of five patterns for this book. Three hats, a scarf, and a pair of socks. They all share a skiing theme, and all are perfect for that little bit of extra warmth on the slopes.

Most patterns for beginners are plain and dull. Most patterns aimed at men tend to be even plainer, and even *more* dull. There was a danger then, that these *beginner patterns aimed at men* would end up being the epitome of plain and dull!

I've done my best to avoid that. The patterns here are definitely easy enough for you to handle, but there is enough interest in each one to keep your attention.

The biggest battle a new knitter faces is not difficulty, it's tedium.

A garter-stitch scarf where you knit row after row with no variation, for seven or eight feet, very quickly loses its allure. I can't think why most people start with such a thing. How can you develop a love for what you are doing, if just getting through it feels like such a chore?

All five patterns in the book use the same weight (thickness) of yarn. I've gone for Aran weight. It's chunky enough that you don't feel like you are working with toothpicks, and the joy of thicker yarn is that your projects grow really quickly, which is great for immediate gratification.

I've chosen the Elmet Aran yarn from my good friend Caerthan Wrack of www.triskelion-yarn.com. He is a wonderful dyer, and his colours are strong and bold, and almost seem to glow from within, like gemstones held up to the light. This particular yarn consists of Bluefaced Leicester (which has a great sturdiness to it, and is fantastic for showing stitch definition really well), and Masham, whose natural grey tones give a wonderful depth and richness to the colours dyed over the top.

If, like me, you want to make all the patterns from the book out of the same type of yarn, whether you choose Triskelion Yarn or not, you will need to get hold of four different colours.

You'll get the best results for the patterns in this book from using solid colours, rather than multicoloured or self-striping yarns. (Self-striping yarns create multi-row stripes in your work all by themselves. All you have to do is keep knitting.)

You most certainly don't need to choose the same colours that I did! It's important that you start to get to know what kind of colours you like the most, and what colours might work best in certain situations.

Choose your favourite four colours, decide which pattern you want to make with which one, and get the correct quantities of each, according to the instructions in the following pattern pages.

Four colours? Aren't there five patterns?

Well spotted. All will be explained when you get to the fifth pattern.

GLOBAL PATTERN ABBREVIATIONS

These abbreviations are used in some or all of the patterns in this book. (The term 'global' is used to mean, 'throughout this book', rather than, 'throughout the entire world…')

Stick a bookmark in here, or just this once, you have my permission to turn down a corner—you might want to find this page again really easily.

cm	centimetre/s
C2B	two-stitch, one-over-one cable crossing to the right
C2F	two-stitch, one-over-one cable crossing to the left
cn(b)	cable needle (hold to the back)
cn(f)	cable needle (hold to the front)
dec	decreased
DPN/s	double-pointed needle/s
g	gram/s
in	inch/es
K	knit
KW	knitwise
m	metre/s
mm	millimetre/s
P	purl
st/s	stitch/es
yd	yard/s
Rnd/s	round/s
work even	This is a really useful instruction that simply means 'work the stitches in the established pattern'. So if a stitch presents itself to you as a knit stitch, knit it. Likewise, if it presents itself to you as a purl stitch, purl it. Basically, just knit the knits, and purl the purls!
wyb	with yarn behind
wyif	with yarn in front
[x,x] x times	Work the stitches inside the square brackets the number of times specified outside the square brackets.

BLUE RUN A HAT

Why Blue Run? Well, on the slopes, the blue runs are those that are deemed suitable for the intermediate skier. You may only think of yourself as a beginner—in fact, this might be your first ever attempt at following a pattern—but after getting this far through the book, I'm totally confident that you have enough skills to get yourself off the green slopes and onto the blue!

The hat itself is an oversized, slouchy hat, designed to be worn with style and aplomb. The body features designs adapted from the traditional stitch patterns used in the old fisherman's gansey jumpers. They are simple to follow and execute, being created entirely from knits and purls. (I thought it would be nice to go with these fisherman's patterns, to carry on the manly theme running through this book—oh yes: none of this happened by chance, it's all been thought through very carefully!)

The rather unusual crown shaping on this hat is actually incredibly easy to do, just featuring judiciously spaced, right-leaning decreases (K2tog) every three rounds. They give a flat-ended look to the hat, which when worn with a suitable swagger can be really rather fetching!

Get your needles in your hands and cast on right away!

(I know you're ready, I just need to convince you that you are as well!)

Needles:	I used a ChiaoGoo 4mm circular needle, and my hat was worked using the magic loop technique. If you prefer to use DPNs, or any other style, feel free.
Yarn:	Triskelion's Elmet Aran 10-ply: 100g = 160m (175yd). 75% BFL, 25% Masham. I bought one 100g skein of the Vincent's Clouds colourway.
Gauge:	My gauge with this yarn and these needles is 20 sts / 30 rows = 10cm (4in) in stocking stitch worked in the round. Gauge measurements were taken laid flat and unstretched (before blocking).
Yardage:	Finished hat weighs approx. 89g, using approx. 142m (156yd) of yarn.
Notions:	Tapestry needle for weaving in ends. If you want to use stitch markers to delineate the repeat sections, you can. The repeats are only 8 stitches wide, though, so I imagine you'll probably be okay without. (You'll need 12 markers if you do decide to use them—remember that a loop of scrap yarn with a knot in it will do the job very well.)
Size:	The Blue Run hat is deliberately supposed to be oversized for slouch and style, as well as comfort and warmth. As knitted fabric is really stretchy, it's a one-size-fits-all kind of hat! My hat measures 24cm (9½in) in diameter, laid flat and unstretched, and comfortably fits around my own, generously proportioned head, which has a circumference of 58cm (22¾in).
Techniques:	Casting on, joining to work in the round, knit, purl, K2tog.

PATTERN

CAST °N AND BRIM

Using the knitted-on cast on described in Chapter 5 (see page 44), cast on 96 sts.

Join to work in the round, being careful not to twist your stitches.

Rnds 1–10: [K2, P2] all the way around the hat.

(If you are using stitch markers, on Rnd 10, place one marker after every 8th stitch.)

NB: If you want a little bit of practice slipping the markers as you come to them, you can always place the markers on Round 7 or 8, and by the time you get to the hat body section, you'll be very used to slipping them from the left needle to the right, whenever you come to them.

HAT B°DY

For the body of the Blue Run hat, I have provided charted instructions *and* written instructions.

Follow only one set or the other. (I would *always* advocate the use of the chart, so that you can get used to how reading a chart works.)

CHARTED INSTRUCTIONS

Remember what you have already learnt about reading charts (pages 126–128). This chart is worked in the round, therefore all of the rows are read from right to left. Start at the bottom—with the row labelled '1'—and work your way up.

The 8-stitch width of the chart makes up one pattern repeat. You will work 12 repeats to complete one round of the hat.

Rnds 1–37:   Work Chart rows 1–37.
Rnds 38–51:   Work Chart rows 1–14.

Row	8	7	6	5	4	3	2	1
37	●				●			
36	●	●			●	●		
35	●	●	●		●	●	●	
34	●	●	●	●	●	●	●	●
33								
32	●	●	●	●	●	●	●	●
31								
30						●	●	●
29					●	●	●	
28				●	●	●		
27			●	●	●			
26		●	●	●				
25	●	●	●					
24	●	●						●
23	●						●	●
22								
21	●	●	●	●	●	●	●	●
20								
19			●				●	
18		●		●				
17	●		●		●		●	
16		●		●				
15			●				●	
14								
13	●	●	●	●	●	●	●	●
12								
11	●						●	●
10	●	●						●
9	●	●	●					
8		●	●	●				
7			●	●	●			
6				●	●	●		
5					●	●	●	
4						●	●	●
3								
2	●	●	●	●	●	●	●	●
1								

Key:

☐ Knit

● Purl

WRITTEN INSTRUCTIONS

If you have worked the hat body from the charted instructions, skip the written instructions, and jump to the Crown Section.

Rnd 1:	Knit.
Rnd 2:	Purl.
Rnd 3:	Knit.
Rnd 4:	[P3, K5] 12 times.
Rnd 5:	[K1, P3, K4] 12 times.
Rnd 6:	[K2, P3, K3] 12 times.
Rnd 7:	[K3, P3, K2] 12 times.
Rnd 8:	[K4, P3, K1] 12 times.
Rnd 9:	[K5, P3] 12 times.
Rnd 10:	[P1, K5, P2] 12 times.
Rnd 11:	[P2, K5, P1] 12 times.
Rnd 12:	Knit.
Rnd 13:	Purl.
Rnd 14:	Knit.
Rnd 15:	[K1, P1, K3, P1, K2] 12 times.
Rnd 16:	[K4, P1, K1, P1, K1] 12 times.
Rnd 17:	[K1, P1] to end of round.
Rnd 18:	Repeat Rnd 16.
Rnd 19:	Repeat Rnd 15.
Rnd 20:	Knit.
Rnd 21:	Purl.
Rnd 22:	Knit.
Rnd 23:	[P2, K5, P1] 12 times.
Rnd 24:	[P1, K5, P2] 12 times.
Rnd 25:	[K5, P3] 12 times.
Rnd 26:	[K4, P3, K1] 12 times.
Rnd 27:	[K3, P3, K2] 12 times.
Rnd 28:	[K2, P3, K3] 12 times.
Rnd 29:	[K1, P3, K4] 12 times.
Rnd 30:	[P3, K5] 12 times.
Rnd 31:	Knit.
Rnd 32:	Purl.
Rnd 33:	Knit.
Rnd 34:	Purl.
Rnd 35:	[K1, P3] 24 times.
Rnd 36:	[K2, P2] 24 times.
Rnd 37:	[K3, P1] 24 times.
Rnds 38–51:	Repeat Rnds 1–14.

Continue to Crown Section.

CROWN SECTION

Rnd 1:	[K6, K2tog] 12 times. *84 sts*
Rnds 2–3:	Knit.
	NB: This is TWO COMPLETE rounds.
Rnd 4:	[K5, K2tog] 12 times. *72 sts*
Rnds 5–6:	Knit.
	NB: As is this.
Rnd 7:	[K4, K2tog] 12 times. *60 sts*
Rnds 8–9:	Knit.
	NB: And this.
Rnd 10:	[K3, K2tog] 12 times. *48 sts*
Rnds 11–12:	Knit.
	NB: Yawn…
Rnd 13:	[K2, K2tog] 12 times. *36 sts*
Rnds 14–15:	Knit.
	NB: …
Rnd 16:	[K1, K2tog] 12 times. *24 sts*
Rnds 17–18:	Knit.
Rnd 19:	[K2tog] 12 times. *12 sts*
	On this round, remove any markers as you come to them.
Rnd 20:	K2tog 6 times. *6 sts*

FINISHING

The crown of this hat is closed using what I call the 'bum-hole bind off'. You'll see…

Break the working yarn, leaving a 15cm (6in) tail for weaving in.

Thread the tail onto a tapestry needle and pass it through the remaining 6 sts, in the direction of your knitting. Remove the knitting needles and pull the remaining stitches nice and tight. Take the tapestry needle through the tiny hole in the centre, to the inside of the hat. Turn the hat inside out, and weave in the end as invisibly as possible. Bum-hole.

Weave in the other end, left hanging where you started the cast on.

Block gently, if necessary, to even out any discrepancies in your knitting.

Wear and enjoy your Blue Run hat.

SKI LIFT A SCARF

This scarf, like the Blue Run hat (see pages 146–149), mostly employs combinations of knits and purls to give texture, but it also includes a simple yet effective cable running along the centre to add a bit of interest and to spice things up for the new knitter.

Why Ski Lift? The chequerboard design of knits and purls reminds me of the construction of an Alpine log cabin, and the sinuous cable running down the middle puts me in mind of a cable-car ski lift, cutting through the mountains as it transports its skiers to the top, ready to start their exhilarating descent.

The best feature of this design, however, is the fact that it is 100% reversible. I have designed it so that the eight stitches that make up the cable are worked in 1x1 rib. This kind of rib looks the same on both sides, but more than that, the act of cabling bunches the stitches up together so that you really can't see the purl ditches between the columns of knit stitches at all.

The squares of the basket-weave patterning are completely regular, and the whole design is framed by a moss-stitch border allowing the scarf to lie nice and flat.

Every single element has been chosen with total reversibility in mind, making this a very wearable scarf, as well as an attractive one.

Needles:	I used a ChiaoGoo 5mm circular needle.
Yarn:	Triskelion's Elmet Aran 10-ply: 100g = 160m (175yd). 75% BFL, 25% Masham. I bought three 100g skeins of the Aneirin colourway.
Gauge:	My gauge with this yarn and these needles is 18 sts / 23 rows = 10cm (4in) in moss stitch. Gauge measurements were taken laid flat and unstretched (before blocking).
Yardage:	Finished scarf weighs approx. 277g, using approx. 443m (485yd) of yarn.
Notions:	5mm (or thereabouts) cable needle. Tapestry needle for weaving in ends.
Size:	My finished scarf measures 20cm (8in) in width, and 192cm (75½in) in length. You can make your scarf as long or as short as you like, however, depending on the number of repeats you work, or the amount of yarn you have. *Just a hint though, leave yourself with about 35g (55m/60yd) of yarn at the end of your scarf. I'll tell you why later.*
Techniques:	You will need to know how to cast on. I have used the 'knitted-on' cast on, as described in Chapter 5 (see page 44).

The border of this scarf is made from moss stitch, but you don't need to remember what that means, as every stitch is charted out for you individually and specified explicitly in the written instructions.

Knitting and purling. That's all. There are no increases or decreases in this pattern.

Cabling: There is only one type of cable used in the Ski Lift scarf. I call it the C8B(rib), and it uses eight stitches in total. The stitches of the cable create a 1x1 rib, and the steps for the cable are as follows:

Step 1: Slip 4 sts, PW, to the cable needle.
Step 2: Hold the cable needle at the back of the work.
Step 3: [K1, P1] 2 times. (Work these stitches from the left needle as normal.)
Step 4: From the cable needle, [K1, P1] 2 times.

Then continue knitting as per the written or charted instructions.

Casting off. I have used the basic cast off described in Chapter 5 (see page 50). Both charted instructions and written instructions are given for this pattern. Once again, I urge you to use the chart.

NB: It can be tempting, when nearing the end of a long project, to want to hurry up and get it finished. Be aware that this could encourage you to finish the scarf before it really *is* long enough. Most people prefer a longer scarf to a shorter scarf, so don't let impatience tempt you into stopping sooner than you should…

PATTERN

Using the knitted-on cast on described in Chapter 5 (see page 44), cast on 40 sts.

(If using the written instructions, jump to that section now.)

CHARTED INSTRUCTIºNS

Remember that this chart is worked flat. Odd-numbered rows are worked from right to left, and even-numbered rows are worked from left to right. (The row numbers tell you where to start each row!) You will also need to remember to use the WS versions of the symbols on every even-numbered (WS) row.

⋮ Rows 1–10:   Work the chart, starting from the bottom and working upwards.

NB: Because all even-numbered rows begin with a purl stitch, remember to start them with your yarn at the front, before putting the needle into the first stitch.

⋮ Rows 11–18:   This is the repeated section. Work rows 11–18 of the chart, then repeat rows 11–18 as many times as necessary until your scarf reaches the desired length, before moving on to Row 19.

I worked the repeated section a total of 57 times. With my gauge, each repeat added 3.5cm (1½in) to the length of my scarf.

⋮ Rows 19–28:   Work the chart.

Jump to Casting Off section.

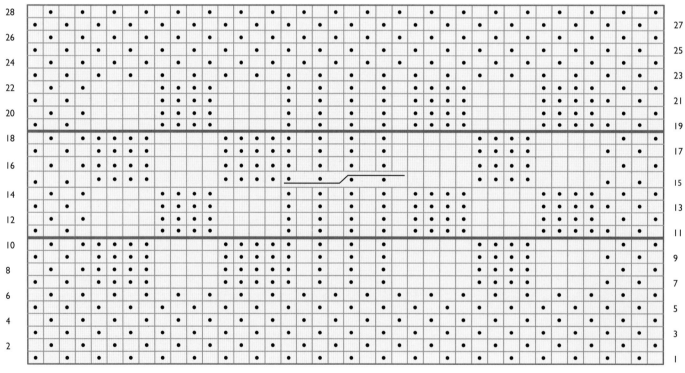

40 39 38 37 36 35 34 33 32 31 30 29 28 27 26 25 24 23 22 21 20 19 18 17 16 15 14 13 12 11 10 9 8 7 6 5 4 3 2 1

KEY:

⬜   RS: Knit, WS: Purl

⬜•   RS: Purl, WS:Knit

•─•─╱•─•   RS Only: C8B(rib) (See Technique Instructions)

═   Denotes the start and end of the repeated section.

WRITTEN INSTRUCTIONS

Row 1:   [K1, P1] 20 times.
Row 2:   [P1, K1] 20 times.

NB: Because all even-numbered rows begin with a purl stitch, remember to start them with your yarn at the front, before putting the needle into the first stitch.

Rows 3–6:   Repeat Rows 1 and 2, alternating.
Row 7:   [K1, P1] 2 times, K4, P4, K4, [K1, P1] 4 times, P4, K4, P4, [K1, P1] 2 times.
Row 8:   [P1, K1] 2 times, K4, P4, K4, [K1, P1] 4 times, P4, K4, P4, [P1, K1] 2 times.
Rows 9 & 10:   Repeat Rows 7 and 8.
Row 11:   [K1, P1] 2 times, P4, K4, P4, [K1, P1] 4 times, K4, P4, K4, [K1, P1] 2 times.
Row 12:   [P1, K1] 2 times, P4, K4, P4, [K1, P1] 4 times, K4, P4, K4, [P1, K1] 2 times.
Rows 13 & 14:   Repeat Rows 11 and 12.
Row 15:   [K1, P1] 2 times, K4, P4, K4, C8B(rib) (remember these cables are ribbed!), P4, K4, P4, [K1, P1] 2 times.
Row 16:   [P1, K1] 2 times, K4, P4, K4, [K1, P1] 4 times, P4, K4, P4, [P1, K1] 2 times.
Row 17:   [K1, P1] 2 times, K4, P4, K4, [K1, P1] 4 times, P4, K4, P4, [K1, P1] 2 times.
Row 18:   Repeat Row 16.

Repeat Rows 11–18 as many times as necessary, until your scarf reaches the desired length, before moving on to Row 19. I worked the repeated section a total of 57 times. With my gauge, each repeat added 3.5cm (1½in) to the length of my scarf.

Rows 19–22:   Repeat Rows 11–14.
Rows 23–28:   Repeat Rows 1 and 2, alternating.

CASTING OFF

Cast off your scarf using the basic cast-off technique described in Chapter 5 (see page 50). Remember that this type of cast off can become very tight, so make sure that you work nice and loosely, without pulling any of the stitches too snugly or the top of your scarf will gather inwards. You might find it helpful to cast off using a slightly larger needle.

FINISHING

Once the knitting is complete, soak your scarf in some wool conditioner to soften the fibres. If necessary, gently block your scarf to straighten out the edges, and even out any discrepancies in your tension. Don't be tempted to block the scarf too aggressively, as you will lose the texture and the thickness built into the pattern.

Once dry, use the tapestry needle to weave in your ends as invisibly as possible, bearing in mind that this scarf is reversible so both sides will be equally visible. Then you can wear, enjoy and be proud of your Ski Lift scarf.

SLALOM A HAT

By now you should be very used to the beginner slopes of our little skiing holiday, and able to whizz down them with ease. It's time to take you out for a bit of a slalom, where you can zig and zag, swooshing this way and that way with gusto.

The Slalom hat is mostly a 2x2 ribbed hat with a wide brim, intended to be cuffed back, giving incredible warmth and comfort across the forehead and over the ears.

Above the brim, the graceful lines of the ribbed columns start slaloming elegantly left and right, joining the lines across the purl gap for a while, before shooting back to their original positions. The overall effect is one of great movement and style.

Needles:	I used a ChiaoGoo 4mm circular needle, and my hat was worked using the magic loop technique. If you prefer to use DPNs, or any other style, feel free.
Yarn:	Triskelion's Elmet Aran 10-ply: 100g = 160m (175yd). 75% BFL, 25% Masham. I bought one 100g skein of the Ynyslas colourway.
Gauge:	My gauge with this yarn and these needles is 29 sts / 24 rows = 10cm (4in) in 2x2 ribbing. Gauge measurements were taken laid flat and unstretched (before blocking).
Yardage:	Finished hat weighs approx. 80g, using approx. 128m (140yd) of yarn.
Notions:	Tapestry needle for weaving in ends.
Size:	My finished hat measures 17cm (6½in) in diameter, laid flat and unstretched. Ribbed knitting, especially at this large gauge, is INCREDIBLY stretchy, and you will find that this hat will fit pretty much any man's head very comfortably indeed. It is not intended to be tight, but nor is it intended to be worn with any slouch. It will hug your head nicely, however big it might be! Incidentally, my own head is 58cm (22 ¾ in) in circumference.
Techniques:	Casting on, joining to work in the round, knit, purl, K2tog, weaving in ends.

There are three different types of cable used in this hat. The first two are just simple, two-stitch cables, crossing to the right or to the left. They are worked as follows:

C2B

Step 1:   SL1 to cable needle and hold at the back.
Step 2:   K1 from left needle.
Step 3:   K1 from the cable needle.

C2F

Step 1:   SL1 to cable needle and hold at the front.
Step 2:   K1 from left needle.
Step 3:   K1 from the cable needle.

The third cable includes a decrease, but is oh-so-simple, there really is nothing to worry about. Here are the steps (all slipped stitches are to be slipped purlwise):

C2FDEC

Step 1:   SL1 to cable needle and hold at the front.
Step 2:   SL1 from left needle to right.
Step 3:   SL1 from cable needle back to left needle.
Step 4:   SL1 from right needle back to left needle.
Step 5:   K2tog.

PATTERN

CAST °N AND BRIM

Using the knitted-on cast on described in Chapter 5 (see page 44), cast on 96 sts.

Join to work in the round, being careful not to twist your stitches.

Now, I know I'm the world's biggest proponent of the chart, but there are times when it just isn't necessary to use one, and this is one of those times. Written instructions only for this bad boy!

Rnds 1–30:   [K1, P2, K1] to end of round. (This gives the same end result as [K2, P2] rib, but I have split the stitches this way so that when you get to the cable rounds, you don't have to worry about working any cables across the end of the round.)

HAT B°DY

Rnd 31:   [C2F, C2B] to end of round.
Rnds 32–38:   [P1, K2, P1] to end of round.

(Remember that because these rounds start with a purl stitch, you need to make sure your yarn is in front of the work before putting your needle into the first stitch.)

Rnd 39:   [C2B, C2F] to end of round.
          (NB: Note that this is NOT the same
as
          Round 31!)
Rnds 40–41:   [K1, P2, K1] to end of round.
Rnd 42:   Repeat Round 31.
Rnds 43–48:   [P1, K2, P1] to end of round.

CR°WN

Rnd 49:   *[C2B, C2F] 2 times, C2B, C2Fdec; repeat rom * to end of round. *88 sts*
Rnd 50:   *[K1, P2, K1] 2 times, K1, P1, K1; repeat from * to end of round.
Rnd 51:   *[K1, P2, K1] 2 times, K1, K2tog; repeat from * to end of round. *80 sts*
Rnd 52:   *[K1, P2, K1] 2 times, K2; repeat from * to end of round.

Rnd 53:   *[K1, P2, K1] 2 times, K2tog; repeat from * to end of round. *72 sts*
Rnd 54:   *[K1, P2, K1] 2 times, K1; repeat from * to end of round.
Rnd 55:   *K1, P2, K2, P2, K2tog; repeat from * to end of round. *64 sts*
Rnd 56:   [K1, P2, K1] to end of round.
Rnd 57:   *K1, P2, K2, P1, K2tog; repeat from * to end of round. *56 sts*
Rnd 58:   *K1, P2, K2, P1, K1; repeat from * to end of round.
Rnd 59:   *K1, P2, K2, K2tog; repeat from * to end of round. *48 sts*
Rnd 60:   *K1, P2, K1, K2tog; repeat from * to end of round. *40 sts*
Rnd 61:   *K1, P2, K2tog; repeat from * to end of round. *32 sts*
Rnd 62:   *K1, P1, K2tog; repeat from * to end of round. *24 sts*
Rnd 63:   *K1, K2tog; repeat from * to end of round. *16 sts*
Rnd 64:   [K2tog] 8 times. *8 sts*

BUM-H°LE BIND °FF

(To be honest, I just like putting those words in large type!)

Break the working yarn, leaving a 15cm (6in) tail for weaving in.

Here comes another bum-hole bind off.

Thread the tail onto a tapestry needle, and pass it through the remaining 8 sts, in the direction of your knitting. Remove your knitting needles and pull the remaining stitches nice and tight. Take the tapestry needle through the tiny hole in the centre, to the inside of the hat. Turn the hat inside out, and weave in the end as invisibly as possible.

Weave in the other end, left hanging where you started the cast on.

Block gently if necessary, to even out any discrepancies in your knitting.

Wear and enjoy your Slalom hat.

APRES SKI A PAIR °F S°CKS

It's time, gentlemen.

You've conquered the manly art of knitting, and persevered through a gazillion tutorials. You've battled your way through umpteen failed attempts. If you're still with me, and still having fun, I think it will be fair to say that I've succeeded, and you will probably be a knitter for life. The moment has come for you to take the final leap of faith and tackle your first pair of socks!

After all, I, your trusty tutor, who has steered you unflinchingly through the rough rapids of this odyssey thus far, am known the world over as *Sockmatician*. I started my own knitting journey with socks, and now it's your turn. It will be my privilege to pass the sock-knitting baton on to you, the next generation of sock knitters.

Back to the skiing metaphors then: your hard day on the piste is over, and you're back at the lodge, celebrating a triumphant black-run descent, or perhaps more plausibly nursing an embarrassingly bruised backside from a lapse of judgement on the beginner slopes that's best forgotten. Either way, you'll want to get comfortable in front of the fire, with a large whisky (or several) and some great banter with your mates. By this time, your toes may have thawed out, but just in case they are still carved from ice cubes, these toasty-warm, comfortable fireside socks will be just what the doctor ordered.

NB: I should point out that these socks, made as they are from a soft, luxury fibre, won't be the hardest-wearing socks in the world. They aren't meant to be. They are designed to be the perfect bed socks or fireside socks, rather than wellie socks or walking-boot socks.

The bulk of the sock features what by now will be a very familiar rib pattern, and the leg is made deliberately long, perfect for folding double, over itself, for extra warmth around your ankles.

Some people don't like having the texture of purl bumps under foot, so I've inverted the sole of these socks, meaning that the purl bumps are now on the outside, rather than the inside. This makes the inner surface of the foot nice and smooth and also gives the outer surface a little more grip on the polished floorboards of the ski lodge.

The Après Ski socks are constructed using the traditional cuff-down method with a heel flap and gusset, and a centuries-old method for 'turning the heel', that I *might* have improved upon just a little bit. You may not be familiar with the heel flap and gusset construction for making socks, as commercially made and bought socks rarely, if ever, use it. I think they have the best fit of any hand-knitted socks I've ever come across, and are great for men's feet, which often have quite high insteps.

There are a couple of little techniques involved in making a sock that you don't yet know, but fear not: I'll take you through them when we get to that point in the pattern.

A QUICK CATCH UP ºN CºNSTRUCTIºN

To start the whole thing off, the leg is worked in the round.

A flat square—called the heel flap—is then created using only half of the stitches. This bit is worked back and forth.

Then you perform a little piece of knitting sorcery called 'turning the heel', and this creates a little cradle—sometimes called the heel cup—for your heel to nestle into. It also changes the direction of your knitting, so that you can continue onwards into the foot, at right angles from the leg.

Before moving on to the foot, though, you'll need to 'pick up' stitches—and I know you don't know what that means yet—along both sides of the heel flap, so you can work in the round once more. As luck (or 'centuries of knowledge', as I like to call it…) would have it, you now have more stitches than you started with, just at the point where you reach the biggest part of the foot. Bravo tradition!

A few well-placed decreases over the next few rounds will bring you back to your original stitch count, just at about the same point that your foot gets narrower. It's then plain sailing along the foot, until you work some more decreases to shape the sock around your toes. Finally, you close the end of the sock by grafting the upper half of the stitches to the lower half.

This method of sock construction has remained largely unchanged over the years, and whenever I am making a pair of socks in this manner—which is often—I feel most in touch with the generations of knitters who have gone before me, each one making little modifications to improve things to better meet their own needs.

I do the same myself.

Knitting isn't static, it's alive, and we can mould it to our will just as much as we can mould the things we make with it to our own body shapes.

Yeah, I know, this is the pattern part of the book, and not the time for reflective reverie, but I genuinely feel that stuff, and this seemed as good a place as any to share those feelings with you.

Needles:	I used a ChiaoGoo 5.5mm circular needle for casting on and for working the first round of stitches, after which I switched to a smaller set of circs, this time with 3.75mm needle tips. I worked these socks using the magic loop technique, but feel free to use DPNs if you want to ingore everything I said about DPNs ealier on.
Yarn:	Triskelion's Elmet Aran 10-ply: 100g = 160m (175yd). 75% BFL, 25% Masham. I bought two 100g skeins of the Dinas Emrys colourway.
Gauge:	My gauge with this yarn and the 3.75mm needles is 20 sts / 30 rows = 10cm (4in) in stocking stitch. Gauge measurements were taken laid flat and unstretched (before blocking).
Yardage:	Finished pair of socks weighs approx. 138g, using approx. 222m (240yd) of yarn.
Notions:	Tapestry needle for weaving in ends. Two stitch markers, large enough to fit onto your working needles.
Size:	These socks are deliberately relaxed in fit, and oversized for cosiness and comfort. It is more usual to write a pattern like this for several different sizes, but I have gone for simplicity here, opting instead for a one-size-fits-all affair. The ribbed texture is incredibly stretchy, and I reckon these socks will fit pretty much any man out there in terms of foot width. The length of the foot is entirely adjustable to suit your own measurements. If you find at any point that your socks are turning out very much smaller than you thought (new knitters can be quite tight knitters), feel free to use a slightly bigger needle than the one specified for the main bulk of the sock, and that should sort things out for you.

TECHNIQUES

Knit, Purl, and K2tog: you're good with those now, right? You're also fine with joining to work in the round, and weaving in ends.

Slipping a stitch: all slipped stitches in this pattern are slipped from the left needle to the right, purlwise (that doesn't, of course, include the knitwise slips inherent in the SSP, just the stitches where you see 'SL1').

SSK: this is the left-leaning decrease called the Slip, Slip, Knit, covered in Chapter 10 (see page 91).

SSP: remember the purl-side decrease also covered in Chapter 10? That. (See page 94.)

Place Marker: at this point, just pop one of your stitch markers (or knotted yarn loops) onto the right needle. It'll stay there until you come back to the same point on the next round.

Slip Marker: this just means that when you get to the point in your knitting where you placed a marker in a previous round, you transfer the marker from the left needle to the right, in much the same way as slipping a stitch purlwise.

NEW (TO YOU) TECHNIQUES

PICK UP AND KNIT (PU&K)

This is the first of the techniques commonly used in sock knitting (and elsewhere) that hasn't yet been covered in this book. It's simply a way to create new stitch loops in an existing piece of knitting, usually up the side of a flat piece of knitting, but sometimes into a cast-on or cast-off edge.

STEP 1

Insert the tip of the right needle into the space where you want to create the new stitch loop. In the case of these socks, you will be working up the sides of the heel flap, and the space to insert your needle into will show up as an elongated V. You insert the tip of your needle under both legs of the V, going in from the front of the work to the back.

STEP 2

Wrap the working yarn around the tip of the right needle, exactly like working a knit stitch.

STEP 3

Draw the new loop back through the fabric, coming out the way you went in, that is, towards you. Again, this is exactly like a knit stitch, except that instead of using a previously made stitch on the left needle, you are using a hole in the side of the knitting. Unlike working a knit stitch, as the new stitch has not been created using the left needle at all, there is no need to slip anything off from anywhere.

For the purposes of picking up stitches along the side of a heel flap, ordinarily you will pick up one stitch for every two heel-flap rows. When you get to that point you will be able to see the vertical line of Vs that runs up the side of the heel flap. Simply start with the one closest to your right needle tip each time, and work into each V as you come to it, until you have reached the other end of the heel flap. (Incidentally, each V encompasses two heel-flap rows, so you work into every V.)

If you find you have misjudged where to begin, and you can't pick up the correct number of stitches, either because you have run out of Vs to work into or because you find that you have some Vs left over, don't worry: undoing the picked-up stitches is really easy.

Just slide the right needle out of the stitches that you want to undo, being careful not to go back too far, and then pull on the working yarn. Those new loops will all unravel, but because they weren't made from live stitches, nothing else will undo. Then you can start picking up once more, hopefully, from the correct place.

You'll come across an instruction to 'PU&K 1 extra st in the corner'. At the top of the gusset section of a sock, there is a little corner between the top of the heel flap, and the line of gusset decreases. This is a notorious spot for getting a hole in your knitting.

STEP 1

Once I've picked up all the stitches I need along the side of the heel flap, I find that picking up an extra stitch in that corner really helps. With these corner stitches—there will be one on each side of the sock, near your ankle bones—it helps to insert the tip of the right needle into TWO spaces, one on the heel-flap side of the danger zone, and one on the same side as the top of the foot, going under two separate strands of yarn.

STEP 2

Then I wrap the working yarn and draw the new loop through both picked-up parts, effectively drawing the two sides of the hole together.

KITCHENER STITCH

SCAN T° WATCH
MY 'KITCHENER STITCH' VID

This pattern uses Kitchener stitch to graft the toe of the sock closed, joining the stitches from the top half of the foot to the stitches from the bottom half. Kitchener stitch is like a little bit of magic. It is a way of grafting two pieces of knitting together, where both edges to be grafted consist of live stitches. Grafting in this manner, rather than sewing, ensures that the texture of the stocking-stitch fabric remains unbroken and continuous. It also means that you are not left with the ridge of a seam, which can be very uncomfortable at the toe of a sock.

It is done with a long tail of yarn on a tapestry needle. You pass the yarn through the loops of the stitches, crossing from one side to the other, creating a brand new row of knitting between the two pieces. The journey of the new yarn accurately mimics the path of any other row of knitting, and if done well, you shouldn't be able to see the join at all.

You need the same number of stitches on each needle for this graft, as you will be joining them together in pairs. It might, therefore, be a good idea to check that you do, in fact, have the right number *before* you begin grafting—undoing a graft is a *real* ball ache!

After a little set-up manoeuvre to start, the graft itself has only a few simple steps, and you'll soon get the hang of it.

Once you have finished knitting the toe of your sock, break the working yarn, leaving a 30cm (12in) tail, and thread that tail onto your tapestry needle.

TIP

For future grafting endeavours, it's really useful to know how much of a tail to leave: there needs to be enough to complete the graft comfortably, but not so much that you have loads left over. Working a graft with yards and yards of surplus yarn gets very dull indeed. A general rule of thumb is that your tail needs to be about four times the width of the graft, plus a little bit extra for safety. So, if you are grafting across a 5cm (2in) piece of knitting, you want to leave about 20cm (8in) of tail plus a little bit more. 24cm (9½in) will be plenty, and you won't face the stress of playing 'Yarn Chicken'.

THE SET UP

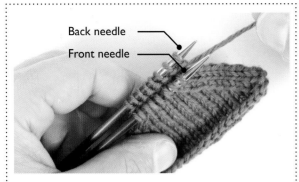

Back needle
Front needle

STEP 1

Position your needles so that you are holding them parallel to each other in your left hand, with the needle tips pointing to the right. Looking down at your needles, you have a front needle (the one that is closer to you) and a back needle (the one that is further away from you). You should be able to see that the back needle is the one that holds the last stitch you worked, and that the working yarn is coming from the stitch on the back needle, nearest to the tip.

STEP 2

Using the tapestry needle, go into the first stitch on the front needle, *PURLWISE*, and pull through.

STEP 3

Go into the first stitch on the back needle, *KNITWISE*, and pull through. That's it for the set-up. You can now move onto the graft itself.

THE GRAFT

STEP 1

Go into the first stitch on the front needle, *KNITWISE*, and slip it onto the tapestry needle.

STEP 2

Go into what is *now* the first stitch on the front needle, *PURLWISE*, leaving it on the front needle, and pull the yarn through.

STEP 3

Go into the first stitch on the back needle, *PURLWISE*, and slip it onto the tapestry needle.

STEP 4

Go into what is *now* the first stitch on the back needle, *KNITWISE*, leaving it on the back needle, and pull the yarn through.

To keep track of what I'm doing as I go along, I chant the following mantra:

Knit Slip Purl,
Purl Slip Knit.

Keep repeating these four steps, until there is only one stitch left on each needle.

To finish, simply work Step 1 of the graft, followed immediately by Step 3 of the graft (missing out Steps 2 and 4 entirely), and pull your working yarn through so that everything is nice and snug.

In an ideal world, you want your grafted stitches to be the same size as the stitches above and below them, so that you can't tell which row was created by the graft, and which rows were knitted. As this graft will be right on the end of the toe, I don't think you need to worry too much about visibility. While it's still new to you, I would err on the side of caution and make sure that you pull the graft quite snugly after each Step 2 and each Step 4. When you have done a few socks, and are used to how it all feels, you'll get better at judging how much tension you need to keep all of your stitches nice and even, but that will all come in due course.

Time to get on with actually making your sock. Ready? Let's dive in.

TIP
When you come to weaving in the end after you finish Kitchenering your toe (yes, I'm using it as a verb), leave the tail threaded on the tapestry needle, and take it through to the inside of the sock.

Make sure that you don't put the needle into the same hole that the yarn is coming out of. It's best to go into the hole *right next to* where the yarn comes out, and that will stop the end of your graft from coming undone.

Then you can turn the sock inside out and weave the end in tidily.

Or not so tidily.

Who is ever going to see it? It's inside a sock…

Or don't bother to weave it in at all if you can't be arsed—it's your sock!

PATTERN

CAST ON AND LEG
Using the 5.5mm needles and the knitted-on cast on described in Chapter 5 (see page 44), cast on 40 sts.

Rnd 1: Using the 5.5mm needles, [K1, P2, K1] to the end of the round.

DISCLAIMER
The cuff of a sock needs to have a lot of stretch in it. This is because it has to go over your heel/ankle, which is the largest part of your foot. The knitted-on cast on isn't particularly stretchy, and it is not the cast on that I would ever normally use for a cuff-down sock. (For the record, socks can be worked both from the cuff down, or from the toe up.)

Ordinarily, I use the German Twisted Cast On, and it works brilliantly well, but I haven't taught that in this book and I wanted to make sure that you can make these patterns just from the contents of these pages, without having to go elsewhere for reference. (If you're interested in the German Twisted Cast On—sometimes called the Old Norwegian Cast On—check it out on YouTube.)

That's why you are casting on with such large needles, to make sure that there is enough yarn in each stitch so that it won't be a struggle to get the sock on!

You now need to switch to your smaller needles. If you are using fixed circulars, just start using the smaller one as your new working needle. Your stitches will automatically get worked from the larger needles to the smaller needles as the round progresses.

If you are using interchangeable tips, and both sizes of tip can be attached to the same cable (some sets have different cables for the larger needle sizes), you can unscrew and replace both tips before beginning the next round.

Rnds 2–70: Using the 3.75mm needles, [K1, P2, K1] to the end of the round.

If you can't be bothered counting your rounds until you have completed 70 in total—and I HATE counting large numbers of rounds—don't worry about it. Just keep going until your sock leg reaches about 23cm (9in) in length. At this point, the exact number of rows isn't really important.

HEEL FLAP (WORKED FLAT)

Row 1:   [SL1, K1] 10 times, turn.

(This means that you are to turn your work at this point, and work the next row on the WS, going back the other way. The rest of the stitches in the round will just hang out where they are for a bit, having a cigarette and a hot chocolate with their mates. You'll come back to them soon enough.)

Row 2:   SL1, P19, turn.

Repeat Rows 1 and 2, alternating, until you have worked 20 heel-flap rows in total.

HEEL TURN (WORKED FLAT)

Row 1:   [SL1, K1] 4 times, SL1, P2, K2tog, K1, turn. *1 st dec*

Row 2:   SL1 wyif, K3, SSP, P1, turn. *1 st dec*

Row 3:   SL1 wyb, P to 1 stitch before the gap, K2tog, K1, turn. *1 st dec*

Gap? What gap?

Don't worry, you'll see it. It's a really obvious space between one stitch and the next, and you knit until you get to one stitch BEFORE the gap, then move on to the next stitch, which is worked across the gap.

Row 4:   SL1 wyif, K to 1 stitch before the gap (yes, it's there on both sides…), SSP, P1, turn. *1 st dec*

Repeat Rows 3 and 4, alternating, a further two times each. *32 sts remain: 12 heel sts and 20 instep sts*

Now, as I do every time I get to this point, sit back, and admire the little piece of engineering wizardry you have just created. Spectacular, isn't it?

GUSSET SET-UP ROUND (WORKED IN THE ROUND)

SL1 wyb, P5, adjust needles so that subsequent rounds will start at this point.

P6, PU&K12 sts along the edge of the heel flap, including one extra in the corner, to eliminate those pesky gusset holes, place marker, [K1, P2, K1] five times, place marker, PU&K1 st in the corner, then PU&K11 sts along the side of the heel flap, P6. *56 sts*

GUSSET

Rnd 1:   P10, K to marker, sm, work even to marker, sm, K to last 10 sts, P10.

Rnd 2:   P10, K to 2 sts before marker, K2tog, sm, work even to marker, sm, SSK, knit to last 10 sts, P10. *2 sts dec*

Repeat Rnds 1 and 2, alternating, a further 5 times each. *44 sts*

Rnd 13:   Repeat Rnd 1.

Rnd 14:   P to 2 sts before marker, K2tog, sm, work even to marker, sm, SSK, P to end of round. *2 sts dec*

Rnds 15–16:   Repeat Rnds 13–14. *40 sts*

NB: Do not remove markers—you will need them again later.

FOOT

This is the bit that will decide whether your sock fits well or not. You have to judge when it's time to move on to the toe section. Remember that knitted fabric gets shorter as you stretch it laterally, so when it looks like your sock is long enough already, it probably isn't! The only way to know for sure is to try it on and see how long it really is once the fabric is stretched around your own, actual foot. (Don't be tempted to try it on with any socks on underneath: that's just lazy, and it will affect the fit!)

I usually end up trying on my socks after almost every round when I'm nearing the end of the foot section. Too often won't hurt. Not often enough will mean a sock you never want to wear. What a waste!

Rnd 1:   Work even. That's it, just knit all the knits, and purl all the purls.

Repeat Rnd 1, until the foot of your sock reaches to 3.5cm (1½in) short of the end of your big toe, while you are wearing it.

TOE

K10, adjust needles so that subsequent rounds will begin here, and remove the marker.

There should be 20 sts between this point and the other marker, and 20 sts between that marker and the end of the round.

Rnd 1:   K1, SSK, work even to 3 sts before marker, K2tog, K1, sm, K1, SSK, P to last 3 sts, K2tog, K1. *4 sts dec*

Rnd 2:   K2, work even to 2 sts before marker, K2, sm, K2, P to last 2 sts, K2.

Repeat Rnds 1 and 2, alternating, a further 4 times each. Remove marker on the final round. *20 sts*

Break working yarn, leaving a 30cm (12in) tail for grafting.

Thread the tail onto your tapestry needle and graft the end of the toe closed using Kitchener stitch.

Weave in your ends, *and don't forget to make a second sock!*

PICKING UP THE PIECES A HAT

Carrying on my skiing theme, you might be worried that the name of this hat is suggesting that you've taken a bit of a tumble in the snow! Don't worry: read on, and all will be revealed.

The fifth and final pattern in this book is included for a very good reason. Oh, you might think you've got the hang of hats now, and I'm sure you have. So why have I chosen to design another one? Well, apart from the fact that a man can never have too many woolly hats, have a look at the photos of this hat. Notice anything familiar about it?

No, not me, you fool! It has been knitted entirely from the scraps of yarn left over from making the other four patterns. Not only will it go well with the socks and the scarf as a bit of a set, even better than that: it's a free hat!

What's not to love about that?

There is another reason. Men often compartmentalise things in their heads and can sometimes find it hard to be flexible with certain ideas. 'I bought *this* yarn to make *this* scarf with. I've *finished* the scarf. There's yarn left over. But I bought it for *this* scarf. There's not enough to make anything else with it. I'd better throw it away.'

STOP!

The more stuff you knit, the more bits and pieces of leftover yarn you'll end up with. Save them. As time goes on, you'll accrue enough scraps to be able to put them together and make something entirely new, just from your leftovers. Using mismatched bits and pieces is not only rewarding because you are essentially getting something

for nothing, but you can also create wonderful effects out of colours you might never have chosen to put together.

I wanted to introduce the idea of a scrappy project, as I know it's something that you might not have thought about doing automatically. There are many patterns available out there that have been put together specifically for using up scraps of yarn, and sometimes, even the tiniest amount can be used as a little colour accent in something larger. So, don't forget to hold on to your odds and sods!

This particular hat has been designed for using up the four colours used in the other patterns in the book. I was left with varying amounts of yarn, and the amounts I used in the hat are specified below. I made the brim with the leftover sock yarn, the main body of the hat was made from the same yarn as the scarf (which is why I said to save a bit, instead of making the scarf as long as it could have been...), and the other two accent colours were scraps from the Slalom hat and the Blue Run hat.

If you don't have the same amounts of yarn that I was left with, or you want to make a two- or three-colour version of the hat, feel free to improvise with how you combine the colours in your own hat. Instructions are given for how to achieve the same results that I did, using four colours, but there's nothing stopping you from adding in more if you have them. Just make sure that all the yarns you choose to include are approximately the same thickness.

I wanted a nice simple pattern that's incredibly easy to make, but with enough visual interest and impact to be really impressive to look at. I'm really happy with the result.

Needles:	I used a ChiaoGoo 4.5mm circular needle, and my hat was worked using the magic loop technique. If you prefer to use DPNs, or any other style, feel free.
Yarn:	Triskelion's Elmet Aran 10-ply: 100g = 160m (175yd). 75% BFL, 25% Masham. I used leftover scraps of four different colourways: Aneirin, Ynyslas, Dinas Emrys, and Vincent's Clouds.
Gauge:	My gauge with this yarn and these needles is 29 sts / 24 rows = 10cm (4in) in 2x2 ribbing. Gauge measurements were taken laid flat and unstretched (before blocking).
Yardage:	Finished hat weighs approx. 83g, using approx. 133m (147yd) of yarn in total, divided as follows:

Yarn A (brim—in my case, green):   45g = 72m (79yd)
Yarn B (hat body—in my case, red):   28g = 45m (50yd)
Yarn C (accent colour—yellow):   5g = 8m (9yd)
Yarn D (accent colour—blue):   5g = 8m (9yd)

Notions:	Tapestry needle for weaving in ends.
Size:	My finished hat measures 18cm (7in) in diameter, laid flat and unstretched. Ribbed knitting, especially at this large gauge, is INCREDIBLY stretchy, and you will find that this hat will fit pretty much any man's head very comfortably indeed. It is not intended to be tight, but nor is it intended to be worn with any slouch. It will hug your head nicely, however big it might be! Incidentally, my own head is 58cm (22¾in) in circumference.
Techniques:	Casting on, joining in the round, knit, purl, slip, K2tog, P2tog. That's about it! And a bum-hole bind off, but mostly because I enjoy typing those words…

Oh, and the 'SL1wyb'. I've added this instruction in, because some of the rounds that contain slipped stitches are purl rounds, and when you purl, the yarn is at the front. You need to take the yarn to the back before you slip the stitch, then bring it back to the front to carry on purling. This is just a little reminder. It stands for 'slip one, with yarn behind'.

If your contrast yarn is only being used for two rounds, it's not worth breaking your main yarn. In these cases, you will be instructed NOT to break the yarn, and it can just hang there, still attached to the work, until you need it again. Then you can just start knitting with it, like nothing has happened.

NB: Every time there is an instruction to break your yarn, you should always leave a 15cm (6in) tail for weaving in at the end.

CAST ON AND BRIM

Using the knitted-on cast on described in Chapter 5 (see page 44), cast on 96 sts.

Join to work in the round, being careful not to twist your stitches.

Rnds 1–30 (Yarn A): [K2, P2] to end of round. Break Yarn A.

HAT BODY

Join Yarn B.

TIP

When joining a yarn of a different colour, simply let the old yarn hang where it is, and start knitting with the new yarn. After a few stitches, if you like, you can tie a little knot between the old end and the new end.

This can be a temporary knot, just to keep things together while you knit the rest of the hat, which you can untie when you come to weaving in the ends, or you might find that you like the security of having the knot there permanently.

There are 'no-knot snobs' out there, but I tend to think you should go with whatever makes you feel the most comfortable.

Rnds 31–34 (Yarn B): Knit. (Do not break Yarn B)

Rnd 35: Join Yarn C, [K11, SL1] 8 times.

Rnd 36 (Yarn C): [P11, SL1wyb] 8 times, break Yarn C.

Rnds 37–40 (Yarn B): Knit. (Do not break Yarn B)

Rnd 41: Join Yarn D, [K7, SL1, K4] 8 times.

Rnd 42 (Yarn D): [P7, SL1wyb, P4] 8 times, break Yarn D.

Rnds 43–46 (Yarn B): Knit. (Do not break Yarn B)

Rnd 47: Join Yarn A, [K3, SL1wyb, K8] 8 times.

Rnd 48 (Yarn A): [P3, SL1wyb, P8] 8 times, break Yarn A.

Rnd 49 (Yarn B): Knit.

Rnd 50 (Yarn B): [K10, K2TOG] 8 times. 88 sts

Rnd 51 (Yarn B): Knit.

Rnd 52 (Yarn B): [K4, K2tog, K5] 8 times. (Do not break Yarn B) 80 sts

Rnd 53: Join Yarn C, [K9, SL1] 8 times.

Rnd 54 (Yarn C): [P7, P2tog, SL1wyb] 8 times, break Yarn C. 72 sts

Rnd 55 (Yarn B): Knit.

Rnd 56 (Yarn B): [K3, K2tog, K4] 8 times. 64 sts

Rnd 57 (Yarn B): Knit.

Rnd 58 (Yarn B): [K5, K2tog, K1] 8 times. 56 sts

Rnd 59: Join Yarn D, [K4, SL1, K2] 8 times.

Rnd 60 (Yarn D): [P2, P2tog, SL1wyb, P2] 8 times, break Yarn D. 48 sts

Rnd 61 (Yarn B): [K1, K2tog, K3] 8 times. 40 sts

Rnd 62 (Yarn B): [K3, K2tog] 8 times. 32 sts

Rnd 63 (Yarn B): [K2, K2tog] 8 times. 24 sts

Rnd 64 (Yarn B): [K1, K2tog] 8 times, break Yarn B. 16 sts

Rnd 65: Join Yarn A, K2tog 8 times 8 sts

Rnd 66 (Yarn A): P8.

BUM-HOLE BIND OFF:

Break Yarn A, and thread the tail onto a tapestry needle. Run the tapestry needle through the 8 remaining stitches, going in the direction in which you have been working. Remove the knitting needles. Pull the working yarn as tightly as you can, to close the hole. Pass the tapestry needle through the centre of the hole to the inside of the hat. Turn the hat inside out, and weave in all the ends.

Soak and gently block, if desired, to even out any discrepancies in your knitting. Wear and enjoy your Picking Up the Pieces hat.

WHERE NEXT?

You should now have a really good understanding of lots of the basics of knitting.

With a bit of luck, an interest has been awoken, and you will be hungry for more. Or at least, you've had a chance to hone your skills, perhaps by completing the five patterns right here or simply by making a few swatches and trying out the various techniques I've talked about.

You might now be wondering where to go to find out more.

THE INTERNET

There is a wealth of information and resources online. Anything you could ever want to know about knitting can be on your screen at the click of a button. We have access to so much more knitting knowledge than in days gone by.

RAVELRY

Your first port of call should be www.ravelry.com. It is the one-stop shop for all things knitty. It is a social media site—dare I say, a 'social knitwork' where you can find forums and join groups relating to every aspect of the fibre-craft world. You can also browse through and download any of hundreds of thousands of patterns, some for purchase and some for free. All my own patterns are available through Ravelry, on 'Sockmatician's Sock Shop' #JustSaying

Ravelry is a great place to find advice, ask questions, learn about what's hot in the world of knitting and who the current designers, dyers, and yarn producers are. Anything, in fact, that relates to your new-found interest is right there for you on Rav. It's also completely free, so you should definitely sign up right away and join the world's largest online fibre-craft community.

SCAN HERE TO
VISIT RAVELRY

YOUTUBE

Probably the second-best resource out there for the curious/adventurous knitter. When I was starting out, I turned to YouTube again and again. You'll find thousands of free knitting tutorials, covering probably every stitch and technique you could ever need to know about. I myself have many tutorials on my YouTube channel (www.youtube.com/sockmatician), so if you feel comfortable with my teaching style and want some continuity, that's one place to look.

My advice with YouTube is this: always watch at least three different tutorials on the same subject, if possible, from three different teachers. With the best will in the world, there are some tutorials out there that get things slightly wrong. Not deliberately, of course (and obviously not *mine*…!), but if you blindly accept everything that is fed to you, you could end up taking those errors on board as fact, purely because you don't yet know any different.

SCAN HERE TO VISIT
MY YOUTUBE CHANNEL

Also, different people have different ways of doing the same thing—as well as different ways of teaching—and it's a good idea to find the way that works for YOU, as I keep saying, rather than try to force yourself to do something someone else's way, purely because it's the only way you've seen. Watch as many videos as you can and choose the method that suits you and your knitting style the best.

Some people will demonstrate a particular technique using their own knitting style. They may be a Continental knitter, holding the yarn in the left hand, while you may be an English flicker, like me, holding your yarn in the right. That may not cause you any problems at all, but you might need to see it being done in your own style to properly understand what they are doing. Again, knitter's choice.

CRAFTSY

There are also many paid-for courses that you can take online. Craftsy (www.craftsy.com) is the leading resource, and you can purchase detailed and *in-depth courses* from expert tutors in many different subjects. There's bound to be a Craftsy course to suit you.

You can also sign up for Craftsy Unlimited, where, for an annual subscription, you can get access to all of the Craftsy courses available. That doesn't just cover knitting, but many other crafting topics as well.

IN REAL LIFE

For a lot of knitters, all they could ever want can be found on the web. Others, like me, enjoy meeting people out and about. There are lots of real-world scenarios where you can find yourself among other knitters, no doubt all of whom will know something you can learn from.

YOUR LOCAL YARN SHOP

One of the best things that you can and *should* do, is start a personal relationship with your LYS. That stands for 'Local Yarn Shop', and there is bound to be one near you.

Unlike a lot of shopkeepers, the people who work in yarn shops tend to be there because they are passionate about knitting (and/or crochet, but I'm focussing on the knitting, obvs). Most LYS owners will be only too happy to chat to you and offer useful advice on what yarn would be good for a certain project, what needles to use, etc.

I have no doubt at all that they will be delighted to help you with any problems you might have encountered. In many cases, you might be able to take your knitting into the shop, with whatever mistakes you have made, and they will gladly advise you and show you how to fix things, so that you can plough on with confidence.

Don't feel self-conscious: although it is true that the majority of LYS owners will be female, I promise you, they will be MORE than thrilled to have a 'guy' knitter walk through the door and will no doubt bend over backwards to help. (Don't be surprised, however, if they initially assume that you are there to buy something for a woman in your life. I get that *all* the time…)

CLASSES AND WORKSHOPS

Most LYSs offer classes on various techniques too, so if you want to learn about Fair Isle knitting, or double-knitting, or making socks, or working magic loop, there will no doubt be a class that you can take somewhere nearby. Learning with a teacher physically in the room is best! Online resources are great, but to my mind there is no substitute for being able to say to a real person, 'look at this, am I doing it right?'

SOCIAL GROUPS

Your LYS will probably also host a regular 'Knit and Knatter' meet-up, or an afternoon 'Craft and Cake' session, where local knitters will get together for a gossip, and the chance to share ideas and inspire each other. These events tend to attract a very wide variety of abilities, so you will no doubt be able to glean a lot of tips and tricks from some very experienced knitters. My own local Knit Night is held in the pub. Marvellous.

My personal experience has shown me that knitters are rarely selfish with their knowledge. Nothing makes a knitter happier than knowing that someone else is showing an interest in what they do, and nine times out of ten, a knitter will want to pass on what they know a little more enthusiastically that you might have expected. But don't be alarmed: that sort of reaction is common among people who spend a lot of their time breathing in yarn fumes, and you'll soon get used to it…

You never know, there may even be a specific Men's Meet-Up near you, where you can relax in the company of like-minded guys, all into the same thing.

YARN SHOWS

A yarn show is like an expo for yarn lovers. They happen all over the world. In the UK, I don't think there is a single month that goes by where a yarn festival isn't happening somewhere. They can be huge affairs, like the massively popular Edinburgh Yarn Festival, or much smaller, more local shows like the Waltham Abbey Wool Show, but all are great fun. Some will even have live animals there, so you can get up close and personal with the sheep breed that provides your favourite fibre (Bluefaced Leicester, in my case), or you might be able to make friends with an alpaca.

There is usually a marketplace—If you can't buy yarn, what's the point of going?—with loads of stalls hosted by independent yarn dyers and providers of knitting equipment, and many shows will offer workshops and classes on a wide variety of techniques. Classes at shows tend to have slightly more pupils in them than classes at your LYS, but the learning experience is just as valuable.

Loop, my local LYS, in Angel, London. Aren't I lucky?

WHO'S WHO IN MEN'S KNITTING?

There is no doubt that the world of knitting is predominantly a female environment. Male knitters are out there, and in some number too, but we are still in the minority. If you have enjoyed the male perspective in this book, you might be interested to know which other guys are out there, among the movers and shakers.

Stephen West (*westknits* on Ravelry) is definitely the biggest name in men's knitting design at the moment. His patterns focus on construction and colour, more than the intricacy of a certain stitch design, and there seems to be no end to his popularity with male and female knitters alike.

Jared Flood (*brooklyntweed* on Ravelry) is the designer behind the popular design and yarn brand, Brooklyn Tweed. His speciality is in cabled garments, and in more traditionally structured pieces than Stephen's more art-based, freeform style, but there's no denying the quality and skill in his work.

Don't forget me! Known across the web as *Sockmatician*, I'm passionate about getting the double-knitting technique out to the masses, teaching classes all over the world, and my portfolio of published designs in books and magazines in the UK and the US is steadily growing. I also host my own hugely popular knitting podcast on YouTube.

Apparently, I've also got a book out…

Other designers to watch out for:

Lars Rains (*modernlopi* on Ravelry) who carved out his own niche by designing traditional Icelandic yoked sweaters but has since taken them in his own direction;

Josh Ryks-Robinsky (*swordofaknitter* on Ravelry), famed for his masculine, geometric colourwork shawls;

John Dunn-Ballam (*easyknitter* on Ravelry), whose inventive and surprising designs always pop with fantastic colour—Jon is also the dyer behind www.easyknits.co.uk, and provided the yarn for all the olive green samples pictured in this book;

Alasdair Post-Quinn (*fallingblox* on Ravelry), double-knitting expert extraordinaire, and one of my personal heroes. Some of Alasdair's patterns are staggeringly mind bending—you'll marvel at their complexity and beauty, and wonder how all that cleverness can possibly fit in just one head.

This little lot alone have enough material out there to keep you busy for decades. It's not all easy stuff, by any means, but I guarantee you'll be looking at some of their designs before too much longer, and instead of saying to yourself, 'I have no idea how to do that', you'll be smiling with the thrilled anticipation of an imminent new project to cast on, saying, 'I wonder what the first stitch in that pattern is?'

IN CONCLUSION

Here's my biggest piece of advice, and this is more important than anything else I have said so far:

THIS BOOK IS ONLY THE FIRST STEP:
DO NOT TREAT IT AS GOSPEL!

It's possible to find peace, meditation, frustration, warmer hands and feet, perfect gift opportunities, friendship, knowledge, learning, community, and a whole host of other things in the world of knitting.

Or you might just want to be able to make a hat.

And that's okay too.

It isn't possible to put everything into just one book. Trying to whittle down all the tiny things that I have picked up over the last seven years has been an almost impossible task. So, by default, this book ain't perfect, and it *certainly* ain't the whole story!

Lots of knitting books teach the basics, as I have, and expect to become a reference guide to return to, time and time again, fixed and immovable.

I don't want that.

Now that you have taken everything you need from this book, I want you to do me a favour. Throw it away.

Yes, that's right: toss it behind you, cast it off dismissively (pun intended), knowing that YOU are the one in charge of where your knitting takes you from now on, not me.

Whatever happens next, I shouldn't be steering you any more, spoon-feeding or dictating what you should be learning. I'm not in your head, so I can't possibly know which bits of this book have inspired you the most. It's time to go it alone.

I've equipped you as well as I can. I've armed you with a little bit of knowledge.

More than that, I've given you a glimpse though the door to Willy Wonka's Chocolate Factory.

And better still, I've told you where he hides the key…

WH° IS S°CKMATICIAN?

The man behind Sockmatician is a knitter called Nathan Taylor.

Nathan started out life as an actor, and has a string of West End musical theatre credits to his name.

To celebrate the first day of same-sex marriage in England and Wales in 2014, Nathan and his husband, Benjamin Till, wrote the music and lyrics for their actual wedding ceremony, which was broadcast in the form of a musical film for Channel 4, called *Our Gay Wedding: The Musical*. The pair won three international film awards for their efforts, and were nominated for a further nine, including a BAFTA.

In 2016, the duo teamed up as writers again, in an experiment for Sky Arts, to see if humans and computers could collaborate to write a hit musical. The process was chronicled in the three-part documentary called *Computer Says Show*, and the resulting musical, *Beyond the Fence*, had a limited run at the Arts Theatre in the heart of London's West End.

Nathan has been knitting in a serious kind of way since 2011, after being bullied by friends to take up the needles. Since then he has released a large number of patterns, and been published in many magazines and books in the UK and the US. He is passionate about double-knitting, and teaches classes on this versatile and beautiful technique all over the world.

His dastardly plan (to take over the world, one double-knitter at a time) looks like it might be coming to fruition…